CW00556356

A Mediator's Musings

on Mediation, Negotiation, Politics and a Changing World

John Sturrock

Copyright © John Sturrock QC 2020

All rights reserved. No part of this publication may be reproduced, distributed, or transmitted in any form or by any means, including photocopying, recording, or other electronic or mechanical methods, without the prior written permission of the publisher, except in the case of brief quotations embodied in critical reviews and certain other non-commercial uses permitted by copyright law.

However, after that official wording, flexibility is important! Do feel free to ask for permission to use excerpts if you wish.

Please write to:

Core Solutions
10 York Place
Edinburgh, EH1 3EP

info@core-solutions.com

John's blogs are published on:
www.core-solutions.com

Cover and text design by Ainsley Francis
www.ainsleyfrancis.com

Index

Introduction 1

Reflections 3

    It Takes Just One Moment for Things to Change, for Good or Bad . . 4

    Mediation and Cups of Tea 6

    Kindness and Courage 8

    What's the Point? 10

    Neil Armstrong Called it on Information Overload 12

    Belief in Excellence Will Take You Far 14

    How Well Do We Perform in Making Scotland a Better Place? . . . 16

    The Abuse of Power Must Be Understood, Not Just Condemned . . . 18

    Paddling Against the Current: Embodied Conflict 20

Negotiation 25

    A Negotiation Emergency? 26

    Process and Empathy 27

    Knowing How to Negotiate Is an Essential Life Skill 29

Mediation 31

    If it Looks Like Mediation?
    And Other Ramblings.... 32

    It's Not Just About the Money
    and Other Food for Thought for Mediators 34

    Never Give Up: Perseverance In Mediation – And Life? 37

Optimising the Use of Joint Sessions in Mediation. 40

Mediation: What Makes the Difference? 42

Mediating Minimally 44

Mediator "Fairness"? 46

Moving to Mediation Makes for Earlier Resolution 48

Mediation: A Cricketing Metaphor. 50

Mediation's a Bit Like Riding an Electric Bike 53

Still Set on Making Mediation Mainstream 55

The Edinburgh Declaration of International Mediators 57

Politics 59

Mediator Engagement in Politics –
and in Other Things We Care About 60

A Universal Declaration of Interdependence is Needed 64

The Certainties of the Past
Will No Longer Afford Security in the Future 66

Civility in Politics Should Not Be Too Much to Hope For 69

Post Election Reflections 71

Mediation in a Changing Climate? -
From Consensus to Confrontation? 72

A Changing World 79

Love Over Fear – and Holding on to Hope 80

World Leaders Must Set Aside Rivalry to Fight This Scourge 82

Communication More Important Than Ever 84

Introduction

I have been attempting to write a proper book for a number of years. I have at least three of them partially written. While I find out whether I am able to complete such a task, this volume is an effort to share some of my thinking a bit more widely. I've selected pieces of my writing from over the past two or three years and arranged them in some sort of thematic order. I think, however, that this is probably a book to dip in to and out of as you wish. I have made a few very small changes to make some pieces more relevant over time. I hope you will enjoy it.

I derive real pleasure from writing short pieces, whether in blog post form or as newspaper articles. I am always pleased when someone says they have enjoyed something I have written. I try to capture a sense of how we might be feeling about things; whether in general, in the world of politics or, more often, in mediation and negotiation and in how we try to resolve conflicts.

I'd like to thank, in particular, Anna Howard and David Lee. At Kluwer and The Scotsman respectively, each has, over the years, encouraged me to write and they have been supportive of my attempts to do so. Without Anna and David, I doubt that what follows would exist at all!

John Sturrock
Edinburgh
March 2020

I'd also like to dedicate this to my family with whom, over the years, I have shared and continue to share a wonderful journey. All proceeds from this book will go to cancer research, in recognition of the speedy and effective way in which our daughter Jennifer's recent cancer diagnosis was dealt with.

Reflections

*"Why didn't we have this
conversation some time ago?"*

It Takes Just One Moment for Things to Change, for Good or Bad

It took just a moment in time: 6 August 1945 at 8:15am. The first atomic bomb to be used in warfare exploded 600 metres above Hiroshima. The city was destroyed in an instant. An estimated 70,000 people died in that same instant. At least the same number again died as a result of the effects, although the number is probably much higher.

To stand at the spot which is "ground zero" in Hiroshima is a moving experience; to view the grim exhibits and listen to the testimony of survivors at the memorial museum is frankly shocking. It brings home the fragility of human existence. It took just a moment.

In Japan, the tea ceremony is a much-loved tradition. Its founder, Sen no Rikyu, offered an explanation of its importance in one simple phrase, ichigoichie: one time, one meeting. Or, put another way: each moment is unique; each moment occurs only once. It will not happen again. Therefore, every encounter, every meeting, must be deeply cherished.

The tea ceremony has a ritual to it, in which the host serves the guests with humility and courtesy. Guests' enjoyment is paramount.

In Japan, much emphasis is placed on according importance to "other people" regardless of age, gender or status.

The principles which apply to the tea ceremony include harmony, respect and calmness. Imperfection and asymmetry are often referred to. Everyone is treated equally in the tea ceremony room. Simplicity, restraint, dignity, gracefulness, mindfulness, non-judgment, selflessness and the connectedness of all things are at its heart. It is about living in the moment. There are particular techniques performed, in a very specific way, and the setting is important too, as is the frequent bowing to one another.

Living in the moment. Hiroshima shows what can happen in just a moment when human beings are set against each other. The tea ceremony captures the idea of the moment in a quite different way, where the emphasis is on building good and respectful relationships.

As someone whose career has focused on helping people to build better relationships and to reduce unhelpful conflict, these ideas resonate with me. As a mediator, I am aware of how important the early meeting of disputing parties on a mediation day can be. Very often I invite the participants to meet together with me for breakfast. The idea is to use the sharing of simple food to create or restore working relationships which will underpin the negotiations which lie ahead that day. I try to set the tone with some remarks about the purpose of the meetings and the behaviours which, in my experience, tend to work well. This may be against the background of previous difficult exchanges, either directly or in a court process.

Reflecting on this moment in mediation, it occurs to me that the principles of the Japanese tea ceremony have application here, and indeed more widely. Respect, dignity, humility, seeking harmony, restraint, non-judgment; these are all helpful attributes in a productive negotiation, whether carried out in mediation or more directly. After all,

each negotiation moment happens only once.

Some of those charged with political leadership in this country might do well to employ this thinking too. And to remember how quickly, in an imperfect world, things can degenerate in human affairs. It takes just a moment.

I have written before about the tension between travel, carbon footprints and facing up to climate change. Recent experience suggests to me that we must find ways to continue to get to know and learn from each other around the world. We will not survive if we cut ourselves off from others. Travel seems essential to our common understanding. We need to find a balance, however, and be discerning and restrained – and to cherish every encounter when we do meet others at home or abroad.

Originally published in The Scotsman on 14 October 2019.

Mediation and Cups of Tea

"If only we'd had this conversation over a cup of tea fifteen years ago." The client expressed frustration at the time which had passed, during which she and her opposite numbers had spent hundreds of thousands of pounds in litigation. That had got them no nearer to solving the underlying problem about which a court action had been raised all those years ago.

Now at mediation, remarkably this was the first occasion the clients had met during that period. Three different court actions, with a fourth pending, had left them financially impoverished and deeply angry at the legal system.

The (fairly recently instructed) lawyers at the mediation could only acknowledge the shocking nature of the situation. There was no rational explanation. Things had got out of hand. That of course had led to the well known problem of sunk costs – and who bears them. There was a possible route to pursue recovery of some of these but it would take that fourth litigation to open that up. Meantime, the real practical issue on the ground still needed to be addressed.

A "cup of tea policy" seems a rather quaint notion. But as a metaphor for meaningful negotiations it works well. Negotiating over a cuppa eases the tension. There is choreography in it too. Mediators can set up these moments well in order to make the very best of the opportunity.

Much more poignantly, the idea of a "cup of tea policy" was proposed at a mediation seminar in Edinburgh last week by Jo Berry, daughter of the murdered British MP Sir Anthony Berry, as an antidote to violence in political conflicts. She did so while sitting next to Patrick Magee, the one time IRA member who planted the bomb which killed her father at the Conservative Party conference in 1984. For seventeen years they have been speaking together about what it takes to overcome hatred and violence and consider healing and reconciliation. The key point they made, though, was the need for real understanding of the "other side". Conversation over a real or metaphorical cup of tea can help achieve that.

"I did not understand where you were coming from." "We felt misunderstood, demonised, not heard properly." "Their political allegiance meant they couldn't see beyond the uniforms..." "Your lawyers didn't even try to make contact to find out what we really needed."

Political malfunction and legal malfunction are not that far apart. For lawyers representing clients in claims handling and dispute resolution, whether in negotiation or mediation, it is critical to make – and take – time to listen and understand as well as to explain and be understood. For mediators, enabling that to happen is one of our primary roles. We must not underestimate its importance.

Originally published in Brick Court Chambers Mediation Blog on 15 November 2018.

Kindness and Courage

Recently, I had the privilege of facilitating a session at Scotland's Citizens Assembly at which politicians from four political parties took the opportunity to discuss with the Assembly members (more than 100 people randomly recruited from across Scotland) their vision for the future of the country.

At the outset, I framed it as a departure from the repetition of partisan political positions. I wanted to explore where parties could work together in the interests of the people of Scotland. It turned out to be an intriguing and encouraging session, with a lot of engagement by the speakers and questions from the members which sought to get under the surface.

As we started, I referred to the Assembly's own "conversation guidelines" and particularly to the call to be kind and supportive to each other. Talking about kindness in a political discussion would normally be dismissed as touchy-feely. But of course, it's not soft at all. It's hard to be kind in the febrile world of debate and denunciation.

A similar thought occurred to me in conversation with a professional colleague just the other day. Suppose we decided that the benchmark for success, a key performance indicator, was how kind we are to others? Suppose the only criterion for an annual review was: "How kind have you been to your colleagues this year?"

Exploring our underlying motivators and drivers is interesting. If it's not kindness, what is it? Is it a need to win? To be proved right? Not to be seen to lose face? To justify ourselves to others? To ourselves? In some recent mediations and facilitations, I have been fascinated to observe the interaction between erstwhile antagonists. It really is as simple, in many situations, as having a respectful conversation. To view the other not as an implacable adversary but as a partner with whom one needs to work in a joint problem-solving exercise. Someone with whom one can do business or restore a worthwhile working relationship. It's how to achieve that which matters.

Which takes me back to kindness. One definition describes "the quality of being friendly, generous, and considerate". It is said that "While kindness has a connotation of meaning someone is naive or weak, that is not the case. Being kind often requires courage and strength."

There's the rub. We often fear being kind because we fear being perceived as weak. The opposite is probably true. To be kind in the true sense of the word is hard, as it requires unusual qualities in today's world. Counter-intuitively, we need to quell the anger or frustration that we feel; to override the reptilian brain's flight or fight response, and find it in our hearts and minds to behave with dignity and courtesy even if the words and actions of "the other side" have disappointed us – or worse.

"Why didn't we have this conversation some time ago?" is a well-rehearsed phrase with which I start many a training day. This expression of regret which I hear regularly in my mediation work really does lie at the heart of things. What gets in the way? Here is where it can get difficult. On too many occasions, I hear it said that "when the lawyers got involved", it all became more adversarial. That could be perception of course. The lawyers often get involved because it has become adversarial anyway and they are then identified with the distress that results. And many, many lawyers in my experience work hard to de-escalate the situation, often in the face of client resistance and demand for tough action. What to do?

I believe the answer lies in that underlying motivation or driver. Is it to act kindly? Or to win? To be proved right? Not to lose face? To justify ourselves to the firm? Can we do our jobs and still be "friendly, generous, and considerate"? To be rigorous about the issues and robust on the problem, while remaining respectful and courteous towards the individuals involved, whoever they may be and however they may act, is the courageous thing to do. If we can do it, we will see better relationships, better outcomes, higher quality solutions and more effective decisions. It's a worthy aspiration.

Originally published in Kluwer Mediation Blog on 29 January, and also published in The Scotsman on 3 February 2020.

What's the Point?

"What's the point?" asked the preacher, rhetorically. "Vanity of vanities, all is vanity" was his text, taken from Ecclesiastes, an Old Testament book apparently attributed to Solomon, whose wisdom we have all heard about over the years. The child and two women each laying claim to being the mother – and all that.

What profit has a person from their labour when the sun rises and falls, the wind comes and goes, the rivers run to the sea? There is, says Solomon, "nothing new under the sun". All is vanity. What's the point?

The preacher had his theological point of course. But even if we leave that aside, what is the purpose of our striving? What are we seeking to achieve? For whom?

Our visit to a church in an island community on the outer edges of Scotland coincided with me also reading Victor Frankl's "Man's Search for Meaning", his visceral account of life, of survival, in Nazi concentration camps. I often quote Frankl at the start of our flagship mediation training courses: "Between stimulus and response there is a space. In that space is our power to choose our response. In our response lies our growth and our freedom."

That observation sits well in a challenging training environment. But what lies beneath Frankl's search for meaning? He said this of "success": "Don't aim at success – the more you aim at it and make it a target, the more you are going to miss it. For success, like happiness, cannot be pursued; it must ensue, and it only does so as the unintended side-effect of one's dedication to a cause greater than oneself...." Frankl draws on Nietzsche: you can bear with almost any "how" if you have a "why". And for each of us it is different: "No man and no destiny can be compared with any other man or any other destiny."

Our preacher summarised our searching by reference to a song by the Irish band U2: "I still haven't found what I'm looking for". Or as Daniel Klein puts it, in his book with this title, "Every time I find the meaning of life, they change it." It could get worse. Our great Scottish philosopher, David Hume, considered that: "The life of man is of no greater importance to the universe than that of an oyster." What, therefore, is the point?

The other day at the Edinburgh Book Festival, I was sitting with Alastair McIntosh, that modern Scottish prophet. Alastair was ruminating about climate change. "I just don't see a solution" he said. We agreed that all we might now be able to do is ask questions and explore options. We also agreed that grand schemes and great fixes may elude us. Perhaps all we can do is do all we can with and for those near to us, we concluded. Maybe that is the point – and that there is a point in that.

Remarkably, in the book by Klein referred to above, he cites Frankl: *"Live as if you were living a second time, and as though you had acted wrongly the first time."* Wise words indeed. What might that mean for those of us who are mediators, often pursuing a second career? What is our purpose? Our cause? Our *why*? How do we define "success"? How do we find what we are looking for?

My good friend, and fellow Kluwer blog poster, Charlie Woods, speaks of our role as guerrilla gardeners, sowing seeds and not knowing where or what might bear fruit. "Have a plan," he says, "and play it by ear". Improvise, be fleet of foot, don't expect to see a return on all your efforts. Funnily enough, the writer of Ecclesiastes said something similar: *"In the morning sow your seed, and in the evening do not withhold your hand; for you do not know which will prosper..."*

Originally published in Kluwer Mediation Blog on 29 August 2019.

Neil Armstrong Called it on Information Overload

At the time of writing, it is more than 50 years since Neil Armstrong first walked on the moon. The release of rare footage in the much-acclaimed film Apollo 11, following on from the movie First Man, reminds us just how extraordinary the achievement was.

In the tributes to Neil Armstrong in Scotland we often hear of his visit to this country in March 1972 to receive the freedom of the town of Langholm, the traditional seat of Clan Armstrong, making it Armstrong's ancestral home town.

Less well known is that, during his visit, he also delivered the Mountbatten Lecture at the University of Edinburgh. Apparently, several overflow lecture theatres with closed-circuit television were needed in the Appleton Tower to cope with the audience of more than 1000 which attended.

The lecture, entitled Change in the Space Age, was remarkably prescient, tracing the history of man's adventures and exploration of the planet and beyond, and anticipating the age of the internet. His theme was the importance, to the collective future of the world, of communication and the transfer of information.

In his lecture, Armstrong observed that, in the past, the flow of ideas was limited to the speed of the traveller, as in the journeys of Marco Polo and Columbus. Then, in the 19th century, things changed with the invention of the semaphore, the telegraph and the radio.

"Man's world would never be the same again," he said. Information could be transferred over vast distances at the speed of thinking. Then computers were developed which could transfer and process information at a speed faster than human thought. Satellite technology enhanced this capacity. Ultimately, for Armstrong, this had led to the remarkable exchanges on his own journey: "Hello, Eagle, this is Houston..."

Looking ahead in 1972, Armstrong anticipated forthcoming innovations – for example, "20 channels of television"!

"One need not cloak oneself in the mantle of the seer," he said, "to predict that we will soon have the ability to transfer any amount of information from any point to any other point at any time." He charted the changes in military command from the battlefield itself to war rooms in Ministry catacombs, distancing the commanders from the field. He observed, referring to the American involvement in South East Asia in 1972, "that remote command may already be a reality." Fifty years later, of course, we have seen unmanned drones become primary weapons of war.

While he acknowledged that it makes the utmost good sense to make decisions at locations where there is most information, Armstrong referred to his own experience of navigating in the remote Sea of Tranquility when, with seconds of fuel remaining, he had to take manual control of, and responsibility for, the lunar landing craft in order to avoid a disastrous descent onto a boulder field. Can "icy logic in another part of the world... replace the experience and intuition of the war horse at the scene of the action?" he asked. In an increasingly AI-dominated world, this question remains singularly pertinent.

In any event, as with direct reporting to the general public from war zones on television, Armstrong reflected that there is a finite limit to human ability to absorb information.

Information overload can lead to a breaking point where we cannot take in any of the facts being presented. He predicted (in 1972) that "tomorrow will bring an ever-increasing bombardment of distilled thoughts, interpretations and visual scenes.

"Complete libraries of books, films, and tapes may become available to the home receiver on request. Satellite service will replace the postal service in many business transactions." Could Armstrong have foreseen the explosion created by the internet, email, Twitter, You Tube and so on...? Would he have cautioned us about the immense amount of information we now try to process each day?

Armstrong concluded his lecture by observing that a great deal remains to be done in the understanding, interpretation, and presentation of information. If that was true in 1972, it is even more true for us now. *"The challenge,"* he said, *"is not merely the accumulation of knowledge; knowledge is not wisdom. Wisdom requires understanding and the key to understanding is communication. Communication is the common denominator necessary to reason, to logic, to explanation, to interpretation. It behooves us all to learn to know and use it well. Our future depends on it."*

Originally published in The Scotsman on 19 July 2019.

Belief in Excellence Will Take You Far

A speech given on the occasion of the Mike (Lord) Jones Excellence in Advocacy Moot at the Faculty of Advocates on 15 November 2019

My title is *World Class Advocacy: Achieving Excellence in What We Do*. I'm grateful to my latest successor as Director of Training in the Faculty of Advocates, Neil Mackenzie, for prompting this title by commenting on the energy, passion and values which he experienced in the early days of the devils' advocacy skills course in the 1990s and which he was kind enough to say that Mike Jones and I exemplified when delivering the course.

World Class – that is certainly what we sought to achieve. In those early days we stood on the shoulders of giants from around the world in developing training here. Mike Jones and I both believed in excellence. Those training courses were the best we could make them.

But what does world class mean? I have had the privilege over many years of working with world class, elite athletes, operating at the highest levels in Olympic and other events. What world class means for them is what it should mean for all performers who aspire to excellence.

It is that extra bit of preparation, the fine tuning of a piece of equipment, the extra mile in every sense, persevering under pressure, standing back and assessing the situation. Focus, clarity, less is more, making a difference in the margins. They say that the difference between mere competence and world class performance lies in those margins.

A tenth of a second on the track, a millimetre above a bar, a pause before striking the ball. Alastair Cook, Johnny Wilkinson, Andy Murray, the list is endless of people who are talented but, much more than that, extract every ounce from each performance.

It's what makes the difference. For Mike Jones as a world class advocate, it was every word being carefully chosen for its task, every question honed to a fine degree, each submission written so that the judge could use it verbatim in her opinion, thinking about the words, actions and visual aids which would create "events in the mind of the audience, in order to persuade". No detail missed.

It comes with energy, passion, commitment to deliver the best. A sense of joy almost, and certainly an appreciation of the values that underscore excellent advocacy, as in elite sport. Not just turning up and playing out a role but whole-hearted participation in the event.

That is what leads to gold medals in sport, success at the highest levels in court and the admiration of your colleagues. Admiration is not necessarily affection. This dedication can place you in the margins, on the edges, not being part of the club. Top advocates have found that. It can be the same in sport.

The Brownlee brothers, Alastair and Jonny, were Olympic gold and bronze triathlon medallists respectively at the London Olympics in 2012. Rather than participate in a more conventional training plan, the Brownlees preferred to do it their way, on their hills. It was not easy.

As the BBC said at the time of their Olympic success: "Do not be fooled into thinking it was anything but brutally hard work. This was not only the culmination of thousands of hours on the bike in the lanes of the Yorkshire Dales, of endless lengths of Leeds swimming pools or miles run around the footpaths and trails of Bramhope, Otley and Bradford,

but of nearly two hours of blisteringly fast, relentless racing under immense pressure."

Peak performance under pressure may be the defining characteristic of the world class performer, be it advocate, athlete, business leader, surgeon or whoever. What happens when it all goes wrong? When you have only a moment in which to make a key, possibly life-changing, decision? How do you react? How do you manage the adrenaline surge? Does your fight or flight (or freeze) reflex kick in?

Or, do you have the resilience, the patience, the physical and mental resources to stay in control, keep calm, consider your options, formulate your words, breathe... even when everything seems lost?

Mike Jones had that resilience and those attributes. For others, thorough training gives us the opportunity to practice the key skills, build resilience, inculcate new habits, change the default setting from fearful anxiety to competent response. And even, on occasion, enables us to achieve world class advocacy.

This speech was published in The Scotsman on 9 December 2019.

How Well Do We Perform in Making Scotland a Better Place?

One of the privileges of my role is that I am invited to do things which give me an insight into aspects of life of which I might not otherwise be aware. Recently, I have been working with the Scottish Leaders Forum Strategic Leadership Group as it seeks to help the public sector and other leaders meet the challenges of Brexit and other events.

In that role, I have learned about Scotland's National Performance Framework (NPF). Developed by the Scottish Government and based on consultations with people and organisations across Scotland, it sets out purpose, values and national outcomes.

By legislation, Scottish Ministers must consult on, develop and publish national outcomes for Scotland and review them every five years. Public authorities must have regard to these. It embeds sustainable development goals and social, economic and environmental indicators designed to measure national wellbeing with a view to enabling all citizens to flourish.

It is designed to be open, transparent and non-political and to encourage a shift from "business as usual". It draws attention to the complex interplay between human stuff and system stuff. It recognises that we live in a VUCA world: volatile, uncertain, complex and ambiguous.

It would be easy to be cynical. More jargon, words, aspirations. However, I was impressed by the ambition and language used.

'Our purpose' is stated to be a focus on creating a more successful country, with opportunities for all to flourish through increased wellbeing and sustainable and inclusive economic growth. Values are identified as being a society which treats all our people with kindness, dignity and compassion, respects the rule of law, and acts in an open and transparent way.

Among the expectations about how the National Outcomes will be achieved, one particularly caught my attention: "We grow up loved, safe and respected so that we realise our full potential." It is not often that we see the word "love" in government policy.

My mind turned to the legal profession. How well tuned-in are our firms and individual practitioners to the NPF? It seems very relevant.

"We have thriving and innovative businesses, with quality jobs and fair work for everyone." Do lawyers tick that box? "We are open, connected and make a positive contribution internationally." Could we do more? "We respect, protect and fulfil human rights and live free from discrimination." How well does the legal profession demonstrate this and ensure that it is a reality for others? "We tackle poverty by sharing opportunities, wealth and power more equally." How many of us contribute to our society in this way? Should we at least ask the question?

I suggest that this is interesting stuff as we join other sectors in facing unprecedented risks in the present and future: inequality, shifting demographics, climate change, environmental degradation, technological disruption, post truth discourse. And so on.

The implications are no different for lawyers. But we may also have something to contribute to wider society. Problem-solving competence, rigorous analysis, communication skills, ability to understand many sides of a story and to get alongside those less skilled and less well-off. Compassion? Kindness? Dignity? Respect? Love? How would we wish to be remembered? Happy Christmas!

Originally published in The Scotsman on 24 December 2018.

The Abuse of Power Must Be Understood, Not Just Condemned

We have heard a lot recently about abuse of power. Most publicly, it has manifested itself in various allegations of sexual misdemeanours in the political and entertainment worlds. It follows scandals about expenses and other misuses of public funds.

These are usually characterised as personal failings and reactions have been highly critical of individuals. In a sense, this is a natural extension of our cultural focus on celebrity. More widely, bullying and harassment, whether physical or mental, are probably endemic, even if often implicit rather than explicit.

These behaviours reveal deep-seated issues about identity, entitlement, status and hierarchies. They may be throwbacks to another age or representative of unconscious biases developed over generations. It is right to focus on them and to seek to reduce their effects in the future.

Critically, however, we also need to understand them. That does not imply acceptance. But underneath the power games will often lie deeper needs, feelings of loss and shame and perhaps downright fear. While there is a natural impulse to blame and shame, that may not address the underlying problems. No doubt that is why lengthy public inquiries are held into serious failings at systemic levels. Whether the present time-consuming and resource-sapping form of inquiry is the right forum to achieve real learning, rather than finding scapegoats and diverting attention for long periods, is another question altogether.

The abuse of power manifests in many ways: curtailing public debate, failing to present full information, redacting documents for self-interest, falsifying key facts, letting political survival trump the national interest, manipulating media reporting, shaping committee membership to influence outcomes, hinting that funding is dependent on curtailing criticism, misrepresenting public views, rewriting independent reports.

These abuses can be harder to pin down. Sometimes those who should call others to account fail to do so or are timid in their pursuit. Often the story does not have enough traction for a media obsessed with personalities. In any event, the same quest for understanding is necessary for these more subtle abuses. Why do people behave, usually collectively, in these ways? What are they frightened of? In the long term, what will the cost be? For how long are we prepared to pay such a cost? How could we do things differently?

These are the kind of questions we will need to pose if we really wish to tackle the more insidious abuses of power in our society.

Originally published in The Times on 5 January 2018.

Paddling Against the Current:
Embodied Conflict

"I've been trying to tell you, but you didn't listen. You've got to go down more deeply and take more time, you're rushing it and it's too superficial. You're hardly disturbing the surface. You'll make no progress that way. And you are using so much effort. Relax. When you get into difficulty, you are expending too much effort trying to change course. It just takes a little adjustment, just row back a little without making such a fuss. It is amazing how quickly you'll adjust to the flow."

"I've been trying to tell you, but you didn't listen". The words came back to me, floating in the air. Familiar words, spoken with kindness and also a hint of frustration. I realised that I hadn't heard them. I was amused by the irony of role reversal. I am usually the person who needs to remind others to listen. But I'd been struggling upstream for what seemed like an age, though it was only about fifteen minutes. I had started off unsure about my position and reluctant to take any risks. As a result, I had not only played safe but tightened physically and mentally, so much so that I felt like I was clinging on just to stay afloat. One or two others tried to help me to regain my poise, but I was reluctant to appear less than wholly competent, even if it

was obvious that I was performing like an amateur on his first stage.

One of the group suggested it might be better for me just to stop now as it would get even more difficult further on. I was unsure, knowing that I was already tired and yet reluctant to admit defeat so soon. So, I was grateful when a senior figure, who had seen it all before, reminded me that perseverance was critical at a time like this, when giving up would have been an easy choice. "You should go for it, I am sure you can do it", he said. Only later did I discover that he was a world expert not only in this field but in another pursuit, even more arduous and demanding of much more courage.

By sticking in and acting on the advice, my first experience of Stand Up Paddle-Boarding became a little more enjoyable. The current was still strong and the wind picked up a little. I got blown about a bit and ran aground twice. But I made it to the end. Indeed, I could have gone on and was disappointed to be told it was time to haul the board out of the river. This, I reflected, is what it feels like to be a beginner in most things. How easy it is to forget where we started out when we have, apparently, become "experienced" and "skilful". How easily our assumed "mastery" can degrade into unconscious incompetence.

These observations will resonate with most of us as we grapple with unfamiliar tasks or feelings of inadequacy. Our reactions under pressure are the result of deeply embedded psychological responses over which we have little control, and which are designed to protect us from danger, however imaginary. My tightening up was borne of little more than fear of getting wet but mirrored the responses that would have been triggered automatically if my life was actually in real danger. Added to the fear of physical threat was the embarrassment of social failure, triggering similar responses. Knowing all of this, theoretically and intellectually, I still could not behave "rationally". And I couldn't hear the very advice offered to save me.

That same day, I found myself exploring a book which helps to explain all of this (and much more) and which could, for me as a "conflict resolution professional", be one of the most important I have read recently. *"Embodied Conflict"* by Oregon mediator Tim Hicks (published by Routledge) is, I suspect, a masterpiece. Sub-titled *"The Neural Basis of Conflict and Communication"* the book's theme is the growing awareness of how our brains work, through many disciplines which include in particular neuro-

psychology and neuro-science, and the fundamental importance, to our collective and individual survival, of understanding all of this – and of improving our ability to prevent destructive conflict in all its forms.

He offers a brilliant reframe: *"It's interesting to think about the violence we see in the world, whether at the level of interpersonal relationships, or at the societal and global levels, as a public health issue."* Could this be the missing link in our conflict resolution field? We've often wondered why what seems obvious to so many of us about how we can better manage and reduce conflict hasn't had the kind of impact we feel it should. Arguably, we have mis-defined it, not fully understanding the depth and breadth of both the challenge and what is needed to resolve it.

Some of us have elevated processes like mediation to ends in themselves. They are, however, merely important examples of means to achieve highly desirable goals. We probably need a much clearer diagnosis and understanding of the underlying conditions, while offering a wide range of remedial steps.

Hicks' recognises that "the success of the conflict resolution field has not only been limited but has not achieved its full promise." He says that "what we call "interest-based negotiations" and "collaborative problem-solving" or, more simply, mediation, can be perceived by parties as risky or threatening for a number of reasons." His exploration of this is too comprehensive to do more than offer an inadequate summary of the main themes here. Indeed, his Preface, in and of itself, is one of the best summaries of the issues I have come across.

Recognising that perceived self-interest, difference, group affiliation and poorly managed conflict is everywhere, the author acknowledges the reality of this and comments that it is our response to differences that create waste and harm, with apparent short-term gains more than offset by longer term and aggregate loss. We struggle with the balance between trust and suspicion, cooperation and competition. Perception, meaning and identity often lie at the heart of conflict.

Our human biography charts our efforts to live more harmoniously in the face of our evolutionary tendency towards fear-based and dominance-seeking responses. Our unique capacity for self-reflection comes with the responsibility to work to change behaviours which are inimical to healthy social life, however we define that. Hicks quotes a philosophy professor: we need to "understand the deep history and tragic complexity of political situations", and with deeper understanding of ourselves, and particularly how and why we behave in response to differences, we can

better prevent or manage inevitable conflicts.

This Hicks offers to do by linking "conflict resolution theory and practice to the basic physiological function by which perceptual experience is encoded in neural structures of meaning." In other words, how the brain works, combined with the experience of the whole body, determines how the mind experiences self and other and how we behave in relationships – and in conflict. The primary question of the book is thus: "How might an understanding of the neural workings of the brain help us work more effectively with parties in conflict?"

In case we are concerned that the author is about to descend into a neuro-psychological black-hole, he reminds us that: "We are biology and chemistry, but we are also our lived experience. In understanding the neural roots of cognition and behaviour, we have to continue to work with people at the level of their and our lived experience. We have to maintain a balance between the science and the humanity of life."

It seems, humbly, to me that, however much some of us in the conflict resolution field may see ourselves as mere brokers of deals, shuttle diplomats or bangers of heads together, such a limiting approach is no longer good enough. If we are to add real value and take this field to where it needs to go, we simply must keep paddling, persevering, trying to acquire greater mastery of the difficult stuff, and overcoming our fear of social failure or appearance of technical incompetence.

For starters, Hicks' Appendix digests specific practical approaches discussed or suggested in the book. But the book as a whole is likely to be essential reading for those who really want to get under the surface and make a real difference.

"I've been trying to tell you, but you didn't listen. You've got to go down more deeply and take more time, you're rushing it and it's too superficial. You're hardly disturbing the surface. You'll make no progress that way."

Tim Hicks' book is a really helpful guide if we choose to listen and go deeper. It will help us to disturb the surface and make progress against the current. We must do so.

Originally published in Kluwer Mediation Blog on 28 July 2018.

Tim Hicks' book made such an impression on me that I wrote about it again in an article published in The Scotsman on 3 June 2019. Here are some excerpts:

Many of us travel to discover more about unfamiliar places, their people, traditions, geography and current politics. It gives us a sense of perspective. On a trip to Alaska, I learned not only about the effects of climate change, but about the indigenous Tlingit people. Despite setbacks, sadness and losses incurred with Western expansion, their culture is being renewed and traditions are being restored. There is a sense of revival. Through greater awareness, sensitivity and acknowledgement by others, their future may be preserved. Travelling brings recognition of our inevitable interdependence in a fragile world.

Crucial to the Tlingit people is their sense of identity, passed on in oral history and traditions. Identity is crucial for all of us in fact, much more than perhaps we realise. And yet identity may be one of the facets of our humanity that threatens us most. In his book, *Embodied Conflict*, the US mediator Tim Hicks describes how our brains are designed to promote tribal activity, with its concomitant inclusion of some and exclusion of others.

Hicks tells us that, for our psychological survival, we seek a coherent and relatively consistent understanding of the world. Yet, in doing this, we can become so attached to ideas, beliefs and knowledge that seem integral to our identity that, whether accurate or not, we will go to extraordinary lengths to defend them. This often leads us to form or join groups – and to ostracise or isolate others. It causes us to take up positions and seek to preserve them, often at all costs.

All we know comes from our five senses, and our interaction with the world. That is where we derive all of our "meaning". We are constantly assessing our environment, responding to and evaluating incoming stimuli to maximise our survival. We are uncomfortable with uncertainty, the unfamiliar, contradictions and paradoxes. We try to fit everything into our familiar picture of the world – or simply deny, dismiss or ignore inconsistent information. All of this leads to construction of a world with meanings that are fraught with inaccuracies, inconsistencies and mistaken biases.

Hicks's insights seem to lie at the heart of many of our current experiences in contemporary politics and social affairs. They also lie at the core of the work of many lawyers who advise clients about how best to resolve disputes or solve problems. Clients will often present with fixed, "correct" views. To what extent do we try to probe under the surface rather than simply reinforcing and supporting that one correct view? How well do we consider the underlying issues of identity when we advise or assist clients? How far do we go to challenge a world view which can only ever be partial?

Understanding the physiology of the brain, and its relationship to perception, the conscious and unconscious mind and our identity will help us (and others) to respond better to differences and disputes. The "new frontier" of neuroscience is the key to this understanding.

Having offered real insight into how we might more effectively understand, prevent and manage conflict, Hicks brings us back to climate change. It is all the same stuff. Both climate change and destructive conflict confront us with ourselves, he says. Both are symptoms of our psychologies, products of millennia of our species' evolution. Both ask us to reflect on our relationships, with each other and with the environment – and on our future trajectory.

Negotiation

"The ability to negotiate well...
is essential to our future"

A Negotiation Emergency?

"For nobody would understand,
And you kill what you fear,
And you fear what you don't
understand."

Powerful words. As a progressive rock music aficionado, these lyrics taken from the song "Duke's Travels" by my favourite band, Genesis, have often brought me up short as I listen to the album from which they come, 1980's "Duke".

"You fear what you don't understand." And you kill it. Whatever "it" is. A person, a group, a philosophy, an institution, an idea.

The lyricist concludes:
"You're on your own until the end.
There was a choice but now it's gone,
I said you wouldn't understand,
Take what's yours and be damned."

Lack of understanding, bequeathing a zero-sum outcome. Be damned.

We are all losers. How familiar is that?

As we head for a "do *or die*" Brexit in the UK, these words have a poignant resonance. Let's kill it. Death is now perceived to be better than working really hard to face the realities of our complex situation. How did we get here?

And what happened to the art of conflict resolution? Where was mediation – or at least a mediative approach? Was it tried? Did it fail? In this most important of issues for post-World War 2 Europe, why did we not Get to Yes? Why have we failed to Get Past No? Where was The Third Side? Did anyone try to Mediate Dangerously? Books with these titles adorn my bookshelves. Must the ideas contained in them always stay there, on the shelf?

The need for a "Conflict Revolution" is clear. We have a Negotiation Emergency at the same time as we have a Climate Emergency. Perhaps mediators need their own Extinction Rebellion.

Originally published in Kluwer Mediation Blog on 28 July 2019.

Process and Empathy

"In negotiations of all kinds, the greater your capacity for empathy – the more carefully you try to understand all of the other side's motivations, interests and constraints – the more options you tend to have for potentially resolving the dispute or deadlock." These are wise words from negotiation guru, Deepak Malhotra of Harvard Business School. He goes on to conclude that *"a lack of empathy usually guarantees failure."*

If these observations were merely academic, we might nod sagely and agree. But they are not. We are hearing more these days about a lack of empathy at senior political levels. Sadly, Malhotra's words may provide at least a partial diagnosis of what has gone wrong with the UK's Brexit negotiations.

In his book, *Negotiating the Impossible*, Malhotra describes three central components of effective negotiation: framing, process and empathy. Another notable writer in this field, Kenneth Cloke, in his latest book 'Politics, Dialogue and the Evolution of Democracy', emphasises the criticality of these components, which he describes slightly differently as content, process and relationships.

Cloke points out that nearly all of our focus in solving political problems is on content while comparatively little time is spent on process and relationships. This may be fatal to solving seemingly intractable issues – like Brexit. Ironically, working hard to build trust and goodwill, being careful with language and showing respect for contrary viewpoints, enhances rather than diminishes the prospects of success. Obvious perhaps. But, to an observer, this doesn't appear to be the experience in Brexit negotiations and we in the UK may suffer the consequences.

As Cloke says: *"when we act unilaterally, in our own exclusive self-interest, in matters that directly and significantly impact others, they feel disrespected and more inclined to resist."* He suggests that if we added up the costs we incur as a consequence, the results would be "staggering" and would vastly outweigh the cost of learning how to talk and act together. Think of the costs already incurred in the UK economy because of the uncertainty arising from Brexit. £600 million per week according to one report. Staggering?

Where does this lead us? Any new negotiating approach to Brexit must, it seems, address these issues of process and empathy. The associated field of neuroscience now reveals much about how we act and react in difficult situations. Surely we need to apply this understanding in the political world? Adversarial, binary approaches which stimulate the fight or flight response (and yes/no; in/out; right/wrong; right/left) may no longer be fit for purpose. We must find ways to deal with complexity, volatility, uncertainty, and ambiguity. We need leaders who understand and can work with these ideas.

This leads to the question of political leadership. The UK's political leaders may have years ahead of difficult negotiations about our future relationship with Europe. Who, of the possible candidates for Prime Minister, has the intellectual and emotional range to handle these negotiations in a way which will ensure constructive political, economic and social relationships?

Adapted from an article published in The Times on 10 June 2019 and a Kluwer Mediation Blog on 28 May 2019.

Knowing How to Negotiate Is
an Essential Life Skill

"The ability to negotiate well, to find ways to cooperate which recognise and promote the broad public interest, is essential to our future. We will not survive without being able to see beyond narrow and partisan positions. Our future depends on being competent negotiators. There is no more important set of skills to teach the next generation."

These wise words from a shrewd observer of recent events resonated this week in Paris at the annual commercial mediation competition for students from universities around the world, hosted by the International Chamber of Commerce (ICC). 66 teams took part from 37 countries, representing every continent and nearly all legal and social traditions. These young people frequently demonstrated negotiation skills and insights well beyond their years and, more importantly, well beyond what we see day today in much public and political life. They recognised that, in order to find solutions to difficult problems, they needed to transcend parochial and polarising positions. They did so with the help of 130 mediators, of which I was privileged to be one, who came from a similarly diverse community of experiences and backgrounds.

I had a mix of emotions. I felt anger about my own generation's failure to exhibit these qualities in sufficient quantity and for having overseen a degradation of civility and loss of respect in recent years. And about the many examples of really poor negotiating skills which are bequeathing to the next generation a legacy of poor outcomes on major issues. I also felt hope for the future as I watched hundreds of young people mingle together and embrace each other, with so much more in common than ever separates them. We need to encourage this as much as we can, at home and further afield.

Suppose we decided that negotiation skills should indeed be a central part of what every young person should learn? What would a negotiation curriculum include? The ICC provides a set of principles to facilitate commercial negotiation, a modified version of which are of general application and which I reproduce here:

• Prepare carefully: define your objectives, purpose, needs and concerns;

• Be aware of (and explore) cultural and other differences and assumptions that exist;

- Identify and agree a process for negotiation, including where you will meet, who will be there and how you will go about it;

- Allocate the resources you need: time, people and technical;

- Develop a good working relationship with your negotiating partner: engage early, learn about what makes them tick, acknowledge what matters to them;

- Behave with integrity: be trustworthy, mean what you say and be clear about your values and what matters to you;

- Manage your emotions: don't be provoked, separate the people from the problem, take care with language both written and oral, and recognise how easily we can all default into fight or flight mode;

- Be flexible: think of creative ways to meet each other's real needs, explore all the options, don't try to secure an advantage which will seem unfair and lead to later difficulties, and make concessions if these will enhance the prospect of an overall agreement;

- Make realistic commitments: be clear about what you can and cannot do and about your and your counterpart's actual authority to agree;

- Confirm and review any agreement reached: check it over, is it realistic, comprehensive, durable, specific and clear?

- Be prepared for the situation where negotiations do not succeed. Having an alternative, and knowing the pros and cons of that, will give you a good benchmark for assessing what you can and cannot accept.

This is all good stuff, even obvious perhaps, for whenever we negotiate. For most of us, that will be every day. To test it out, I invite you, the reader, to take a current negotiation which you have or foresee having. Whether it be a property transaction, an employment problem, a difficult commercial dispute, a family bust-up, a business investment, or the future of your country, work your way through these principles as an exercise. What do yo-u learn? What will you do differently as a result? Can you use them to make a difference? What outside help could you call upon? And how can you help the next generation to learn to use these principles well?

Originally published in The Scotsman on 18 February 2019.

Mediation

"We believe that mediators have a unique role to play"

If it Looks Like Mediation?
And Other Ramblings....

I have been asked to act as an independent third party in two significant matters where the parties (including public sector agencies) have specifically said they do not wish to call me mediator or for the process to be one of mediation. They wish to describe me as a "facilitator". Everything else feels broadly the same, looks broadly the same and requires nearly the same approach. But without formal "position papers", without recognising there is a "dispute" of the litigious sort, and perhaps without the expectation that I shall rigorously test the parties on their positions. It's been interesting and, in some ways, seems to free the parties up to be more experimental, less adversarial.

I can't say more for reasons of confidentiality but wonder if anyone else has this experience? It does not matter much in my jurisdiction where there is no developed jurisprudence or legislation covering "mediation" but what if there was? Does the language matter? Just because we decide to call it "facilitation", does that disapply any legal rules that may be applicable to mediation? Mind you, I often call myself a "facilitator" in workplace/management disputes already; it seems more comfortable for the parties and seems to reduce a fear of formality that even our informal process of mediation can create.

To move on, I recently acted as a mediator in a difficult case where one party (an experienced professional) refused to meet with the other party (a lay person) because the former did not want to "humanise" the latter. His explanation was coherent from his perspective and given his role and objective. For me, the nature of the dispute made a meeting obvious and, from a mediator's perspective, even necessary. It would have helped the lay person enormously. Paradoxically, it would also, in my view, have assisted the professional party. But this was one of those rare instances where to insist on a meeting (not that one could) would have been counter-productive on the day.

Ironically, in another very similar matter, against his instincts, another professional party did meet the lay person. He explained to the lay person (who was accompanied by a lawyer) why the lay person's defence would not work. The lay person explained that s/he needed to hear that explanation, from the horse's mouth as it were, in order to move on and accept certain consequences.

The professional party's lawyer was moved to say to me afterwards that this one of the most powerful meetings he had ever experienced in a mediation. It was a game-changer. It could only have happened in mediation, in a confidential setting where sufficient trust had been built in the process, if not between the parties.

Trust: that essential ingredient in human affairs. As we look towards the election here in Britain, trust seems to have evaporated in a sea of deceit and fake news. Suppose we believe that the biggest concern is how we do politics rather than any particular policy? Suppose we wish to see reform of public discourse and a return of civility in the public square? Suppose we see our politicians as bell-weathers of how society discusses important matters? Suppose how our political leaders act sets the tone for others? Suppose we think that civil discourse in Parliament is the essential precondition of a necessary, mature consideration of what really matters, such as climate change, automation of jobs and mass migration?

What sort of people do we wish to see and hear considering these and other difficult matters? How would we wish them to conduct themselves, and behave towards each other and others, including us, the electorate? We probably know the answers to these questions. Might the answers give us some relevant benchmarks for deciding who to vote for this time round? Can/should we mediators/facilitators encourage people to think this way?

Originally published in Kluwer Mediation Blog on 28 November 2019.

(Note: I learned subsequently that contractual arrangements which refer to "mediation" can be overly formal; "facilitation" can get round this.)

It's Not Just About the Money and Other Food for Thought for Mediators

A number of mediations have reaffirmed some essentials which I share here in the hope that they might be helpful to others:

It's not all about the money. Mr A had a very substantial claim against a bank running into hundreds of thousands of pounds Sterling, most of his life savings. When I asked him, early on, what he needed from the mediation day, he replied "I'd like them to apologise". The bank's advice was that it had done everything it could and that it had no legal liability. A familiar situation. However, the bank's representatives found a way, authentically, to convey their deep regret that Mr A had experienced losses. They said they would do everything they could to ensure it would not happen again.

Mr A was very pleased with what was said. The matter settled for a modest sum overall. The Bank and Mr A conducted the final stage of the negotiations themselves, with support from advisers. Both parties left the mediation process satisfied with the outcome.

When wheels have come off, re-engage the key players. Day two of mediation was designed to build on day one several weeks earlier.

However, the parties had not made the expected progress. In private initial meetings, one party expressed frustration and a feeling of lack of respect being shown by the other party – and a desire to conclude the process and proceed with litigation.

The engagement between the mediation days had been at a level below the key players. When the principals came together in a private meeting with me, they were able to hear from each other about their mutual frustration with what had happened. They agreed that they needed to oversee the process.

Much progress was then made in joint meetings in which the subordinates addressed the main issues under the watchful eye of the principals. The less senior people (including professional advisers) behaved in a different way with each other as they explored why they had not made progress, where the difficulties lay, and what needed to be done to make faster progress. The most senior people watched, asked questions, summarised, and provided guidance and leadership. The parties probably achieved more in half a day than for several months.

Get under the surface. In a long-running claim worth many tens of millions, the decision-makers appeared to have reached the end of the road. In an effort to find a way forward, we spent four hours going through my 'Questions for a Difficult Meeting' questionnaire. The parties prepared privately first and then, meeting together, they alternated in giving their responses. The nature of the questions is such that they needed to dig deeper to look for answers. This opened up new levels of understanding about pressures, outside constituencies, alternative courses of action, changed realities and validation required for amounts sought. It led to a further discussion about possible settlement figures.

Ask questions. Similarly, in a difficult mediation involving very senior directors in a company, impasse had been reached. Or so it seemed. But the more questions I asked, about their own ambitions, what others would say about them, how they might have contributed, what they might change or do themselves to make a difference, what questions they needed to ask, what pressures each was under, what they might be missing, and so on, the more they could see for themselves what needed to happen. I am a great believer in party autonomy. Questions, used well, compel people to take responsibility.

Use a worked example. Many of us struggle with figures. Few of us really get to the bottom of what the numbers are telling us – or might tell us if we understood them. In a mediation involving a business partnership in which property was being divided up in a separation, the lawyers had spent several hours trying to explain what it all meant. Eventually we got the flip chart sheets up and the parties themselves began to map it all out. It wasn't easy as there were so many variables around land valuations, compulsory purchase possibilities and development proposals. And the taxation aspects were uncertain. However, for over an hour, we worked it through.

One of the parties was moved to say: "The figures are so much easier to understand than the lawyers' words"!! Enough said. A satisfactory deal was done.

Encourage forward-looking momentum. When the going gets tough, maintain a process and be clear what that is – and try to ensure that the parties continue to commit to it. It has been said (by Deepak Malhotra in his excellent 'Negotiating the Impossible'): "Stay at the table even after failed negotiations – if you are not at the table, you are on the menu".

The job of the mediator is to (a) try to offer the best possible process for the circumstances; (b) keep in touch with and support parties even when there seems to be an impasse and (c) be prepared for a window of opportunity to open up, perhaps unexpectedly. Keep looking for it. In my experience, it often does. And we rediscover that most people, whoever they are, wish to resolve their disputes by agreement.

Provide food. Continuing with the idea of eating, it is encouraging to have endorsement of the value of bringing all the participants in a mediation together to share food. I do this whenever I can, with everyone meeting for breakfast after my initial private meetings. A buffet lunch can also be useful where people can choose to linger and chat if they wish. (There is academic support for the role of food and a similar point has been made about the important role of glucose levels in decision-making.)

So that will be pizzas for the early evening final push for resolution then! It is all food for thought...

Originally published in Kluwer Mediation Blog on 10 April 2019.

Never Give Up: Perseverance
In Mediation – And Life?

"If you had not held us back that evening, the deal would not have been done."

"Thank you and I wish you well."

In this post, I return to a familiar theme for mediators and for lawyers acting for clients in mediation: perseverance.

The first of the two quotations above comes from a participant in a mediation spread over four days and nearly one year. It was a complex matter involving many parties and some difficult issues. Towards the evening on day four, a proposal from the claimants was met with a lower counter by the defendants. The parties had laboured hard and the claimants felt that they had gone as far as they could go with the process. Or at least some of them did. Two principals left the building along with leading counsel.

That might have marked the end of the mediation. However, I had a sense that there was more to play for. I expressed my frustration with the situation, spoke with those who remained and suggested a further meeting, one to one, involving one of the claimants' key advisers and his opposite number. "Let's give it a go"

was the sentiment. I knew that each were keen to find a resolution and that they respected each other. No lawyers were present.

In that meeting, things were said and options were explored that resulted, three weeks later, in a comprehensive deal settling all matters. Only because we went that extra mile. And, perhaps, in hindsight, it was helpful that the others had left early. They provided the space for someone to step forward who could bring about change in the pattern.

The second quotation narrates the words of the chief executive of a large supplier of services to the public sector. He spoke the words at 9.45 in the morning, less than one hour after the start of the mediation. Breaking with convention, and with the agreement of all concerned, I had arranged to start the mediation with a meeting of the two principals on their own. All of the legal and technical stuff had been well covered by the lawyers in the paperwork: the principals had met previously and they knew each other.

The purpose of the meeting was to explore whether either party would be prepared to move from a previous stalemate. In a friendly and frank conversation, one had explained to the other that, with further inquiries carried out and substantial further costs incurred, he was in fact not even able to start at the previous point. His counterpart responded that, in that event, there was no point in continuing. He departed the meeting with the words set out above.

Four hours later, the parties were drafting a settlement agreement. What had happened? We didn't accept things at face value. We stuck at it. By "we", I mean myself and the two principals, supported by their teams. We continued to explore, to dig deeper, to try to understand what was really going on and what each needed. We reminded ourselves of the cost of the alternatives to a settlement. It was a classic piece of positional bargaining in one respect, each trying to find out how far the other would actually go. But without the structure and safety of mediation and a mediator with whom to talk frankly and confidentially, it is unlikely the principals would have had the ability to reach an outcome. And the lawyers supported them throughout.

What can we take from this? Here are a few observations:

- It is really important not to assume that what the other side say is what they really mean

- Even if it is what they mean at a particular point in time, that may

change for a number of reasons

- Your job (as lawyer/mediator) is to challenge assumptions and keep looking for new angles and ways to see things

- That involves the classic techniques of really good questioning, really keen listening, reframing the words/topics, getting under the surface (again and again), changing the environment and/or the participants, constantly benchmarking against the alternatives, teasing out the various options however obscure

- You must maintain good relationships with all those involved: they are nearly always trying their best and you don't know who may hold the key or act as a tipping point

- And remember the outside constituencies (shareholders, lenders, government officials and ministers, business and life partners) whose needs and interests may be crucial – and therefore to whom you may need to help either party build a bridge.

A final thought: perhaps this is all going on in the Brexit negotiations. I hope so. But I fear not. So many people have suggested that mediators could help. From the examples above, that is probably obvious. So the big question for the next generation is this: how can we ensure that mediation, with all its benefits, is used in high stakes political negotiation as it is in other areas of human activity? It will take much perseverance to get there. But it can be done.

Really, these are all lessons about life itself. One of Scotland's lesser known music groups was a band known as Pilot. They had a lovely little song entitled "Never Give Up", the B side to a number one hit in 1975 entitled January. In the chorus they sang: "Stay to the end, I'm gonna try and I'll never give up". That song remains one of my favourites – and an inspiration in my work.

Originally published in Kluwer Mediation Blog on 28 February 2019.

Optimising the Use of Joint Sessions in Mediation

Much has been said and written about the demise of the joint meeting in mediation. In my experience, such a view is premature and, I fear, is potentially wasteful of the power that mediation brings for creative problem-solving. I am also aware of how much the clients and others appreciate a creative approach to the structure of meetings in mediation.

I illustrate my point with this (somewhat abbreviated) example of a series of meetings in a recent two-party construction-related mediation with independent experts involved. This is not an unusual example in my practice and I am sure others find this too. And this is not a prescriptive template. Much of what is described here is improvised on the day.

The diagram on the next page gives a flavour. The middle column denotes when a meeting involved participants from both parties.

(* denotes occasions when the mediator would pop into private rooms to discuss progress)

This is merely an example. The danger is that we think we know or do it better than others. I hope this may further stimulate discussion on a very important aspect of our practice.

A revised version of this blog was published in the Summer 2018 issue of The Resolver, the quarterly magazine of the Chartered Institute of Arbitrators (CIArb).

		Mediator in private with Party A
Mediator in private with Party B		
		Mediator in private with Party A
	All participants together in main room for refreshments and informal mingling, followed by a welcome and introduction by the mediator, setting out guidelines and the next steps	
	Mediator alone with the two principals (the key decision-making clients) to enable them to exchange views	
	Mediator with the two principals and the two lead instructing lawyers (solicitors) to plan an agenda	
	Mediator, two lead experts, the two principals, four solicitors, selected relevant team members from each party: Party B's expert presents Party B's response to Party A's claim (claim presented in advance)	
Party B reflects in private*		Party A reflects in private*
	Party A's principal alone with Party B's secondary expert and one Party B technical adviser: information gathering on technical issue; held concurrently with:	
	Mediator with in house technical specialists from each party exchanging information, with four solicitors, discussing and seeking to resolve a series of specific quantum issues	
Party B reflects in private*		Party A reflects in private*
	Mediator with the two principals, four solicitors and in house specialists from each party, reporting back on the previous concurrent meetings	
	Mediator, two experts, two principals, four solicitors, relevant team members from each party: Party A's expert presents a response to Party B's expert's comments earlier	
Party B reflects in private*		Party A reflects in private*
	Mediator with the two principals and the two lead solicitors to summarise progress and articulate further action steps and ensure recording of these	
	All participants together in main room for summary by the mediator, thanking all for participation and looking forward to a second day of mediation; handshakes and good humour all round.	

Mediation: What Makes the Difference?

Two different mediations. Each with a completely different subject matter. Different cities. Different months. Different lawyers. One involving a construction contract, the other financial services.

Each reached a stage in negotiations where one party offered an amount, x, and the other party sought an amount, y. Remarkably, the amounts x and y were the same figure in each mediation and thus the difference between x and y was also the same. That difference, in the overall scheme of things, was relatively small, significantly less than 10% of the principal sums. Neither claiming party had a specific need to achieve y. There was an emotional component present for both. The paying party was on each occasion funded by an insurer.

At the end of each mediation, the parties' principals, the clients, met together in an atmosphere of mutual respect and thanked each other for the attempts made to resolve a difficult and long-running matter. The negotiations were, largely, conducted in a spirit of openness and apparent good faith.

And yet....in one mediation, the parties reached an agreement and, in the other, they did not. What was the reason for these different outcomes?

As ever, there is no one answer. One might ask what had happened, if anything, during the day in each case to trigger or prime a certain response? I couldn't detect reactive devaluation. Each party seemed to accept that the other was doing its best. Optimism bias, perhaps, but over such a relatively small difference? Could that really cause a deal to be lost, or a bridge not to be built, when the ongoing court costs would soon exceed the difference?

Possibly the endowment effect: one has so much invested in one's own view of value, that objectivity is hard to achieve. But what about risk aversion? In each case, there was real risk on the facts and good reason to settle. And the bird in the hand theory ("carpe diem") seemed really important, perhaps especially in the case which did not resolve, so that discounting possible future value to achieve present certainty appeared to be a rational thing to do. And yes, costs had been incurred so that the sunk cost fallacy may have had an impact but everyone was also realistic about future cost escalation. This was the time to reach agreement if possible.

There was one factor which may have been material. In one case, the lawyer was quite proactive in carrying out a pragmatic risk assessment and in helping the client to be realistic too. Expectations were managed and any tendency to exaggerate or inflate was resisted. Concessions were offered in order to expedite the negotiations. In the other matter, the lawyer seemed more reactive and willing to leave decisions with the client. There may well have been a different dynamic in that room, a different client-lawyer relationship and expectation – and of course I was not privy to discussions which occurred while I was not present.

Further, my own relationship with the claiming parties was marginally different. My attempts to test reality and check understanding of risk were received in slightly different ways, one welcoming, another less so. When combined with the different approach of the lawyers, that may have created a sense of pressure by the mediator in one matter, which may in turn have created resistance. It is difficult to do other than speculate.

And my sense was that insurer attitudes were quite different. In one case the insurer was personally present. In the other, the insurer was on the end of a telephone. Might that have made a difference?

Incidentally, in the case which did not settle, I subsequently suggested (carefully) that the parties might split the difference but (obviously) only if both wished to do so. To my surprise, that I should even make such a suggestion was met with disapproval by both. Perhaps directing their ire at the mediator would galvanise them. Funnily enough, on my desk that evening, I discovered the book "Never Split the Difference" by Chris Voss. Point made.

Originally published in Brick Court Chambers Mediation Blog on 17 September 2019.

Mediating Minimally

As another year comes to an end, I am expanding upon a recent story, in the hope that it may provide a couple of useful reminders of what we do as mediators.

I had eaten a chicken curry rather hastily at the hotel where I had been mediating the day before, just prior to boarding the overnight sleeper train to London for the following day's mediation. I had settled in fairly well and slept as well as one can in a moving carriage with its usual fits and starts.

However, on waking at about 5.30 am, I felt distinctly unwell. By the time the train had arrived in London at 7.15 and we were due to leave our cabins, I was unable to stand up without an overwhelming sense of nausea. I had not felt so ill for a long time. Eventually, the staff kindly provided a rather primitive buggy to carry me from the train to the first aid post in Euston station, an uncomfortable journey and one which I was unable to complete without renewing my acquaintance with my chicken curry.

In the first aid room, I had the presence of mind to send an email to the lawyers in the mediation which was due to start at 9.00 am, to say that I might be a little late. I

also requested that they secure me a bedroom to enable me to lie down on my arrival (fortunately, we were mediating in a hotel nearby). Fortified with medication from the station pharmacy, I made my way gingerly to the hotel and to my room.

I emailed the lawyers again and suggested that they come to my room separately for our initial private meetings. This they did, rather reluctantly at first, but we avoided any physical contact. Although I was unable to sit up, we had a useful pair of meetings. They were keen to suggest that we should just abandon the day. However, I knew from earlier communications that this was an important matter and that many people's work situations could be affected by what was decided that day. It couldn't really wait. I said I would do what I could and work my way carefully through the day. We agreed to proceed.

I managed to make my way down to the basement conference rooms for the first joint session. While there was sympathy for my circumstances, that did not extend to the parties modifying their views of each other. Opening presentations were as robust as one might have expected. As the morning wore on, I was helped by one principal client calling for a break to attend an urgent meeting. This enabled me to head back to my room and enjoy a warm bath. Taking a bath in the middle of a mediation is a new experience for me and one which I thoroughly recommend. It brings a sense of calm and perspective – as does good anti-nausea medicine.

As the day progressed, the participants were kind about my stamina. In reality, however, they did all the hard work. And it was hard work. The other reality was that had a mediator not been present, the negotiations would almost certainly have broken down in acrimony and with possibly serious repercussions for thousands of people. Indeed, it took an exceptional effort to secure the final breakthrough at about 7.15 pm.

Why tell this story? Well, I learned two things. Firstly, we mediators often feel the need to take on more of the load than is necessary or appropriate. Less is more. I had to conserve my energy that day and play a limited role. I had little choice but to do the minimum I was able – and needed – to do. Paradoxically of course, this enabled (or perhaps compelled) clients and lawyers to take responsibility and make informed choices. Secondly, as I allude to above, a mediator's role, even with minimal intervention, is usually crucial. It provides the necessary third party presence, a watchful eye at least, a calming influence, a degree of accountability for behaviour and, very often, a strategic sounding board, while delivering the extra final push can make the difference in the toughest of situations.

As we move into another year, reminding ourselves of these two central features of what we do as mediators may enable us to achieve even more than we do already in our work. Happy new year!

Originally published in Kluwer Mediation Blog on 28 December 2017.

Mediator "Fairness"?

We recently finished module 2 of our flagship training course. One of our participants emailed me the following day:

"I was driving up the road yesterday and mulling over one aspect of the mediation exercise we did. I get that we are facilitating adults to make fully informed autonomous decisions and that they need to make that decision based on their priorities, circumstances and judgement – that is not the mediators job. Ensuring they can consider all options and think about consequences etc, as well as making them aware they have the opportunity to seek professional advice helps.

However, it was the aspect of "needs" that concerned me. When Paula said she would accept a figure which was more than her immediate need (her debt that needed repaid soon) there was a request for her to consider if that was actually her need or would another figure (probably lower) be acceptable. That would clearly help the mediator get towards an agreement. But would it be fair? Does a mediator need to worry about "fair"?

I like the idea of mediation because it opens up a process that is more accessible than courts. It takes out the size of the wallet as being one of the deciding factors of an outcome as is often the case in court battles. But if we don't consider fairness it does feel that, if you are needing the money, you are more likely to settle for a very small bird in the hand. If Paula didn't have debt she wouldn't feel so pressured to reduce her "wants".

I think I am arguing myself to the position that it is the fully informed autonomous decision that is important and that mediator fairness (or at least the mediator's view of fairness) should probably not be the concern. But I am not sure how comfortable I feel about that. Is it just a fact of life that the more "needy you are" the more likely you are settle for less? Can someone be a mediator when their instinct is to fight for the underdog?"

I replied:

"A great question and one with which many have wrestled over the years, not least those concerned with "justice". And those whose instinct is to fight for "underdogs".

Perhaps, if one's instinct is to fight for the "underdog", then one should be an advocate, not a mediator. That is unless one can somehow set that bias (for that is what it is) aside.

"Fairness" is an elusive concept. What seems "fair" to one may not seem "fair"to another. How do you decide? By making a judgment based on what you know. But what do you know?

Paula may have a "sugar daddy" in his Merc outside. She will not tell you. The organisation may have no money or may go out of business before the Tribunal hearing on Paula's claim. You may not be told.

In any decision, people take account of so many factors, conscious and unconscious. Apparent needs is one. If you test that out and, in particular, test out the BATNAS and WATNAS, what else can you do? Who are you to superimpose your judgement on that of Paula if she is fully capable of making a decision and as well informed as she can be? How would you feel if you said "that's not fair" and a deal wasn't done, and Paula was then assaulted by the drugs guy to whom she owes 10k and who won't be waiting till the Tribunal in x months time? It's not easy.

If handled well, mediation offers an opportunity for people to decide what they want to do in their own particular circumstances. And, yes, the more needy may actually get less in money terms on an objective view. But what is it worth to them? The widow's mite comes to mind. Paula's being "pressurised" is not because of mediation. It's because of her circumstances. Countless people in the court system win and lose because the judge is incompetent or their lawyer didn't prepare well. How fair is that?

So, how can a mediator ever have a "view of fairness" that is anything other than subjective or at least largely irrelevant to the matter in hand?"

This is a provocation. Now, over to you all. Thoughts? Responses?

Originally published in Kluwer Mediation Blog on 1 May 2018.

Moving to Mediation Makes
for Earlier Resolution

As a mediator I look back on my years as an advocate at the Scottish Bar with great affection. The intensive preparation the night before. The pre-court anxiety as one wondered which judge would be allocated. Gathering volumes of case reports from the Advocates' Library. The discomfort of the old courts in Parliament House. Those lengthy cases where evidence was heard over several days or even weeks. Sitting next to and observing the outstanding Queen's Counsel of the day in action. The anticipation while awaiting the opinion of the court, perhaps weeks after a hearing.

Lately, however, reflecting on the cases in which I was involved, I have asked myself: could at least some of these have been mediated, had mediation been available? Then, as now, most cases in the Court of Session settled without being decided in court. In the mid-eighties and into the 'nineties, settlement nearly always took place on the morning the case was due to start. Parliament Hall was a mass of bodies. Clients and solicitors would be looking anxiously at counsel who would be strolling up and down the Hall, in step, discussing the strengths and weaknesses of their cases. This was hardcore negotiation

and there were many masters of the art.

Many of these cases could, and in hindsight probably should, have settled earlier. But the system in those days did not cater as it does now for earlier resolution. Agreement is now reached at earlier stages in many cases. Let's leave for now whether even earlier and/or more satisfactory outcomes could be achieved with mediation.

I am interested in those cases of mine which did go to court. What if mediation had been suggested in the Lands Tribunal cases where I was junior counsel to David Hope QC (as he was), in which we acted for the appellants Exxon and Shell against valuations made by local assessors in respect of the Mossmorran natural gas liquids plant in Fife? Or Hibs, Hearts and Celtic regarding the valuations of Easter Road, Tynecastle and Celtic Park? Could a mediator have been brought in? Probably not, as these were issues of valuation principle with wider application and too much at stake. They probably needed judicial determination.

But what about Balfour Beatty against Scottish Power which reached the

House of Lords? In a case about the continuous concrete pour needed to construct the Union Canal aqueduct over the new Edinburgh bypass, the question was whether it was within "reasonable contemplation" that a blown fuse would lead to demolition of the aqueduct. The case was decided on a point on which, as I recall, there was very little evidence at the first court hearing but which became fairly central in the appeal to the House of Lords. There was risk on both sides and the costs must have been relatively high compared to the sum sued for. It was all or nothing. Nearly ten years elapsed between the event and the final decision. I suspect that it could well have been mediated satisfactorily at a much earlier stage. That would have resulted in one less House of Lords authority of course but I am not sure the parties would have been too concerned.

In another complex matter, I was junior counsel for the pursuers in what was then one of the biggest intellectual property cases, Conoco against Merpro Montassa. This concerned a patent for a hydrocyclone which separated oil and water in the North Sea. We had weeks of evidence and had commenced our appeal when the case settled for commercial reasons. There was much at stake and the outcome was always uncertain. I imagine that mediation, which is now regularly used in IP matters, could have brought about an earlier commercial resolution.

I often recall Mr and Mrs Pickering for whom I acted alone in a judicial review of a planning decision, against both the regional and district authorities, each represented by senior and junior counsel. Although we lost in the first court, there may have been a good appeal point. But the Pickerings did not have the resources to continue. Then, as now, the question arises: could a matter of public law have been negotiated using mediation, to the benefit of all concerned – and saving time and money? Quite possibly. Times have changed.

Originally published in The Scotsman on 15 April 2019.

Mediation: A Cricketing Metaphor

Recently, I was ruminating about analogies between cricket and mediation. Cricket is a much-loved sport in Scotland. Sadly, nowadays, changes in the climate mean that cricket in my home country is more often affected by summer rain and damp conditions than a generation ago. Its future is less certain as a result.

I have always been a cricket fan. Ever since England played the West Indies in 1969, and the great Gary Sobers was still in his prime. When I was in my early teens, I was coached by a kind, talented West Indian professional called Noel Robinson. He played a few seasons for my home cricket club, Stirling County. I learned to bat properly. My cover drive had such a flourish that, in my first year at university, I was selected high up the batting order for the first XI after impressing at practice in the nets. It did not take long, however, for my fear of really fast bowling to be exposed. The 2nd XI soon beckoned.

But it was in defensive play that I excelled, both on the front foot and the back. I practised for hours. I could bat for ages. My schoolmates would be frustrated as I ground away in those 20 over games, collecting singles and accumulating runs at a snail's pace. 39 not out seemed to be my badge of honour. That England legend, Geoffrey Boycott, famed for persevering at the crease, was my role model.

Unlike many sports, for an individual batsman one mistake is all it takes to end participation in the game. A mistake that may result from a moment's inattention. Or a rush of blood to the head. A split second of indecision. A distracting thought. Conversely, sharpened focus, a microsecond's pause, a determination not to let the overall circumstances get in the way of giving complete attention to the next moment, blotting out an earlier near miss – all these promote longevity and continuation in the game.

For a batsman, stroke selection at the critical moment is what it is all about. I recall hearing that the distinction between an average opening batsman (the example given was one Nick Compton, who never quite established himself as an England player) and Alastair Cook (the most successful opener of all time for England) is a tiny fraction of a second. Cook takes that little bit longer before committing himself to his stroke. He takes just a little more time to process, sub-consciously, the bowler's action.

That makes all the difference. How much of that is practice, how much is intuition and how much is personality, I don't know. But this does makes you think.

In mediation, we operate with a mixture of spontaneity, flair, caution and discernment. Often, how we react in the moment makes all the difference. We need to be able to take risks sometimes, or we'd never move the process on. On the other hand, over-playing our own role, letting the ego prevail, can be fatal. It's such a question of balance. Usually, of course, our errors are not decisive. The ball metaphorically drifts past the wicket into the safe hands of the wicket-keeper without snicking the bat or striking a wicket. It can be touch and go at times. We are all human, error prone.

What then sets apart a really effective mediator from the average? For me, it has to include an ability to focus on the process regardless of the outcome, an ability to operate with consummate skill in the moment, knowing that, paradoxically, this will enhance the prospect of a successful result. It has to include a willingness to practice skills, never assuming mastery, with humility about the reality of our role and its importance. I would add awareness of one's own personality and psychology, and of those triggers which might set off a chain of events leading to unhelpful loss of confidence during mediation. It's about standing

back, surveying the field, viewing where the mediation players have positioned themselves, trying to work out where the opportunities lie for getting past unhelpful defences, picking the moment to drive towards a breakthrough.

And being brave enough to allow that extra momentary, fractional pause. A little more time before responding, a little more time to elicit – and hear – an answer and to process the real meaning. Concentration, even when tired at the end of a long day (remember that Alastair Cook once batted for 836 minutes in a crucial match, albeit over two days). An ability to stay engaged, raising your performance when all seems lost and, as with so many of the best sportspeople, seeing unexpected things in one's peripheral vision that others would often miss.

A few seasons ago, my Scottish mediation business, Core Solutions, sponsored the Scotland cricket team. Our billboard carried the eye-catching slogan: "Mediation – There Are No Boundaries". That nicely summed up our adventurous hopes for what we were doing. Mature reflection might suggest that recognition of boundaries is actually necessary too. In cricket, a draw is often seen as an unsatisfactory outcome for both sides, but it can also represent a realistic equilibrium when two well-matched sides have done their best.

In mediation, a negotiated agreement may also seem unsatisfactory if your objective has been victory. However, as we know so well, the optimum result in mediation may be both parties leaving with a sense of dissatisfaction – but knowing that, with this match finally over, a whole new game can start the following day, on a new wicket with fresh opportunity and renewed optimism.

Originally published in Brick Court Chambers Mediation Blog on 27 February 2018.

Mediation's a Bit Like Riding an Electric Bike

"I have been doing this for the last 40 years. I would prefer to continue to do it as I have always done. There's no need for this extra help. In fact, people would think I had gone a bit soft, or that I couldn't manage it myself. And not many people do it anyway. It's more costly too."

This was my response to my wife's suggestion that we should each obtain bicycles with electric batteries. I have cycled with vigour and enthusiasm all my life. The idea I might now need some help to do so was not welcome. I still want to show the world (and myself) that I have the ability to cycle just as I always have. It was lost on me that a different approach might enable us to explore new places, enjoy cycling over longer distances together, expand our travel options, add value to our holidays and share new, enriching experiences.

However, we tried out e-bikes at the cycle shop with the help of an excellent salesman and I began to see that this could be a game-changer. "Go for a ride," he said, "take your time. It's up to you". His experience and quiet authority gave us confidence; enough confidence, as it turned out, to make a purchase there and then.

We took the bikes on holiday and cycled for distances and to places we would never have contemplated under our own steam. The result was longer, tougher, more exhilarating cycle rides in the windswept Outer Hebrides. The penny dropped. This was a game-changer. And then another penny dropped: my experience was probably similar to that of many reluctant to use mediation. We assume change will not be good for us, that we will lose control.

Having a battery on your bike does not mean you don't need to expend effort. You can cycle under your own steam for as long as you wish. You use your gears as normal. You retain complete physical control – and use the power in the battery only when you want to or really need it.

You have choices. On my bike, I have "eco" (minimal additional power, just to help a little when the going gets slightly tougher, making travel a bit more pleasurable), "tour" (for a longer ride, maybe with a good bit of headwind or a gradual incline over hundreds of metres), and "sport" (when you need a good boost in city traffic).

And then there is "turbo": it's a gravel path, the wheels are spinning, the gradient is 1:4 and, frankly, the alternative is to get off and push – or give up. "Turbo" is impressive and can make a real difference just when you need it. But if you rely on it overmuch, it loses its value.

The analogy with mediation is obvious. Mediation is something which still seems new to many experienced professionals. They know what they are doing. They have done it for years. To seek additional help feels like weakness. Mediation looks like an additional cost. It probably feels easier to reject it than take the risk of apparently handing over control to something new and untested.

But of course, in mediation, people still have full control and need to work with considerable effort to make progress. However, they can also utilise a bit of extra assistance from the mediator when things might be getting tough, or to inject some real pace when it is needed. A light touch "eco" mode may be all that is required to ease the negotiations along. If a crisis occurs and the wheels are coming off (or perhaps just spinning too much), the mediator can bring stability and forward momentum to keep the show on the road.

At the end of the day, it is still all about choice. How far to go. What mode to use. How much help to engage. When to apply the brakes and say: enough.

Those who promote mediation need to appreciate that helping people to feel in control is probably critical. Any hint of condescension ("I know what is good for you") wouldn't have worked for us in the bike sale. How many of us have been guilty of over-pushing mediation because we know it is so much better?

Now all I need to do is overcome the embarrassment of powering past those lycra-dressed athletes on racing bikes on Edinburgh hills. And remember to charge the battery...

Originally published in The Scotsman on 26 August 2019.

Still Set on Making Mediation Mainstream

When I was a law student in the late 1970s, teaching on subjects such as housing law, social security and even employment law was a minority activity, if it existed at all. That these topics became mainstream was significantly due to the work of the Scottish Legal Action Group (SCOLAG) whose journal was both radical for the times and a source of information about these and other areas of law. Then, as is still the case now, access to justice was difficult for many who were economically, socially or otherwise disadvantaged.

It was a great pleasure to be invited to celebrate publication of the 500th edition of the SCOLAG legal journal at the refurbished law school in Edinburgh's Old College. Indeed, the main event took place in the lecture theatre where I recall learning the rudiments of consumer credit and other more mainstream areas of law and jurisprudence from the great lecturers of the day, such as Professors Neil MacCormick and Bill Wilson. 17 years since I last made a contribution to the SCOLAG journal, I was invited to write for the 500th edition. My topic was the same: bringing mediation into the mainstream in Scotland.

In that recent article, I mention that, 17 years ago, I had provided numerous illustrations of what seemed to be, in 2002, growing demand for mediation services in Scotland. Then, I had noted that, *"with significant efforts being made over the past 12 months, a large number of those within and outwith the legal profession are becoming more aware of the benefits of mediation - and are showing an increasing willingness to use it."*

So, who would have thought that, 17 years later, I would co-chair an expert group which has published a detailed report recognising that mediation has not so far achieved the impact and uptake in Scotland which we all agree it should have done. The Report comments that the use of mediation in resolving civil disputes in Scotland is currently much lower than might be expected.

While mediation is now used to a greater degree than in the past, the report acknowledges that various efforts over the past two decades or so to promote its benefits have not significantly changed a legal culture committed to litigation. Even where objectively it might appear that parties' interests would be better served by mediating their dispute, the default position is still generally to litigate.

We know that adversarialism is costly. Whether in our justice system, the way we handle disputes generally, national politics or international diplomacy, it seems that we need a more constructive, cost effective and creative way to sort out our difficulties. Mediation provides such a way for many situations.

The report recommends much greater use of mediation in the Scottish civil justice system. It recognises that mediators can help people to find resolution of the most intractable of disputes, where the power to make decisions is restored to the people who really matter. The detailed proposals in the Report point the way to mediation being used to help people to manage and resolve disputes in our communities and businesses, workplaces and families, and indeed more widely.

Coupled with recent proposals for a mediation bill from Margaret Mitchell MSP, the recommendations now emerging in Scotland arguably point us in a more enlightened and cooperative direction. 2019 seems to be the year when Scotland is finally taking the opportunity to bring mediation into the mainstream.

Originally published in The Scotsman on 1 July 2019.

The Edinburgh Declaration of International Mediators

I write this in the aftermath of an extraordinarily uplifting and diverse conference which I had the privilege to host and chair recently in Edinburgh, under the auspices of the International Academy of Mediators.

Nearly 120 mediators from over 20 countries attended and shared deep discussions about how we as mediators can look outward and work towards a "new enlightenment" in the tradition of the great Scottish Enlightenment of the 18th and early 19th centuries. The conference was a seminal moment for Scotland and mediation in our country. The praise from delegates has been universal and unequivocal.

About 100 mediators signed the historic Edinburgh Declaration setting out what we believe in and commit to as mediators. Signing took place in a ceremony in the Scottish Parliament on Saturday 12 May, following well-received addresses emphasising the value of principled negotiation delivered by negotiation expert **William Ury** (fresh from work on the Korean summit) and **Scotland's First Minister**. It is helpful to share the Declaration with a wider audience, as often mediation is not well understood or is viewed restrictively.

Here are some excerpts from what we said:

- We believe that it is in the interests of our world as a whole and our own communities in particular that difficult issues are discussed with civility and dignity.

- We believe that it is very important to find common ground and shared interests whenever possible and to enable and encourage people to work out difficult issues constructively and cooperatively.

- We believe that finding common ground and shared interests requires meaningful and serious dialogue which requires significant commitment from all concerned.

- We believe that understanding underlying values and addressing fundamental needs is usually necessary to generate long-term sustainable outcomes.

- We believe that restoring decision-making and autonomy wherever possible to the people who are most affected in difficult situations lies at the heart of good problem-solving.

- We believe that mediators have a unique role to play in helping to promote the principles we have set out above.

- We believe that it is a privilege to act as mediators in a wide range of difficult situations in our countries, communities and the world as a whole.

- We are committed to offering our services to help those in difficult situations in our countries and communities, and in the world as a whole, to deal with and resolve these for themselves in a constructive and cooperative way.

- We are committed to doing all we can to maintain our independence and impartiality in those situations in which we are invited to act as mediators and to build trust in our work as mediators.

- We are committed to maintaining and raising professional standards through training, continuing development and sharing of best practice.

- We recognise that it is important to exemplify the values that we seek to encourage and, in our work as mediators, we undertake to do our best, and to encourage others to do their best, to:

  o show respect and courtesy towards all those who are engaged in difficult conversations, whatever views they hold;

  o enable others to express emotion where that may be necessary as part of any difficult conversation;

  o acknowledge that there are many differing, deeply held and valid points of view;

  o listen carefully to all points of view and seek fully to understand what concerns and motivates those with differing views;

  o use language carefully and avoid personal or other remarks which might cause unnecessary offence;

  o look for common ground whenever possible.

The Edinburgh Declaration feels like a seminal document. It gives Scotland an opportunity to show leadership in promoting cooperation and thoughtful solutions to difficult problems. Doing so is not easy of course but it seems preferable to the alternatives.

Originally published in The Scotsman on 18 June 2018.

Politics

"There is no us and them, only us"

Mediator Engagement in Politics – and in Other Things We Care About

At an excellent conference hosted by Professor Ulla Glaesser at Viadrina University in Frankfurt (Oder), one of the workshop sessions focussed on the extent to which mediators can or should disclose or express their views when engaged in politically-related mediation work – or more generally.

What a fascinating conversation we had. It was no mere academic exercise either. We had a representative from Ukraine who described the really difficult situations in which mediators could find themselves in that country. Are mediators agents of change or providers of a "service", we asked ourselves?

In his thought-provoking new book, *Politics, Dialogue and the Evolution of Democracy* the legendary Ken Cloke reflects on an exchange between two distinguished American authors, Lawrence Susskind and Bernie Mayer. I quote the passages from Ken's book in full:

"In a recent issue of ACResolution, magazine of the Association for Conflict Resolution, two opposing positions on escalating political conflicts in the U.S. were taken by highly experienced, deeply intelligent leaders in the field of conflict resolution. The first was by Lawrence

Susskind, founder of the Consensus Building Institute at MIT and a professor in the Program on Negotiation at Harvard Law School, writing:

Neutrality is central to the value we add as ADR professionals. Our neutrality allows us to earn the trust of all sides in a dispute... My contention is that many ADR professionals are so upset by what is happening in the Age of Trump that they are ready to risk their neutrality. While I understand their motives, I am convinced this would be a disaster for the profession... If you sign a petition, march peacefully, write op-eds, or lobby for your point of view, there is no way anyone who disagrees with the positions you have taken will accept you as a dispute resolution professional they can trust. I promise you that whatever actions we take in our personal lives will be noted.

A second, contrasting view was authored by Bernie Mayer, a professor at Creighton University and writer of several brilliant, profound and far-reaching books on conflict resolution:

We are, sadly, experiencing the rise of open and unconstrained racism, misogyny, anti-Semitism, and homophobic behavior in our public lives, abetted and even provoked by our President and his associates. Are we obligated to remain silent about this in order to maintain our status as credible neutrals? On the contrary, I think one of the great contributions we can make as conflict interveners is to call out unacceptable behavior, which is making it increasingly difficult for us to talk across our differences or to deal with the most important challenges we face as a society. We need to find constructive and effective ways to confront unacceptable behavior both in our capacity as conflict professionals and as citizens of our world. But we must do this in a way that recognizes that people can change, that interactions make a difference, that people who behave in an abusive manner still have genuine concerns that ought to be addressed, and that we ourselves are fallible.

There is something accurate in both of these statements, yet there is also something I find missing. It should not, I think, be necessary to surrender one's political ideas, beliefs, values, ethics and morality in order to mediate or facilitate dialogues between people with opposing views. Being "neutral" in these conversations should not mean surrendering the freedom to think or have an opinion on important political issues. Otherwise, we capitulate to bullying, blackmail and intimidation, and end up, in the incisive critique of anthropologist Laura Nader, "trading justice for harmony."

On the other hand, "calling out unacceptable behavior" and engaging in polarizing confrontations, while useful in pressuring politicians and calling attention to social injustices, can quickly devolve into pointless name-calling, excessive personalization of political differences, distraction from problem solving, cyclical backlash and over-simplification of complex issues.

What is missing in this discussion is the deeper mediative truth that lies beneath both these statements: that it is possible for us to be open and unbiased without being neutral on issues that matter; i.e., to transcend both bias and neutrality, and work to transform conflict generating behaviors without slipping into unnecessarily apathetic or adversarial thinking."

What a lot of food for thought. Speaking personally, I write regularly for newspapers and other media outlets, offering views on political matters, mostly commenting on process and relationships rather than on the substantive issues. However, in this, I am necessarily drawn into commenting on the behaviour and attitudes of politicians and others. I believe it to be my duty to speak out about these matters. Indeed, as I write this, I have an article in the Scottish edition of today's UK Times, reflecting on my learning in Frankfurt about the impact of Brexit in Europe.

I lead a not for profit organisation called *Collaborative Scotland* which, by definition, promotes a certain way of discussing difficult constitutional questions, especially if framed as "What kind of country do we wish to be?". This is, I suppose, a political question. I have promoted a *Universal Declaration of Interdependence* which may seem to sit uneasily with those who support independence in my country. And yet I argue strongly that there is no inconsistency. It is about how we do things rather than the substantive outcome. But what if I (secretly or even unconsciously) believe that this approach might help to achieve a particular outcome?

And what if a mediator is asked to facilitate negotiations, the very outcome of which will inevitably offend his or her political (or other) beliefs? Take the case of our colleague who has been asked to mediate on the question of where and how many wind turbines should be installed in a particular place, but who believes that no more wind turbines should be installed as we need to reduce energy consumption dramatically. Or the mediator with a gay son who believes that Jesus loves everyone unconditionally and that same-sex marriage should be accepted by the church, and who is invited to mediate between a group of church members who feel passionately that the Bible teaches otherwise and a group which takes a more permissive view.

These may be important questions for us in coming years. And even now, many of us will have wrestled with these sorts of issues in our work.

Interestingly, for me, the only (apparent) consequence of my own activities seems to be that I was judged to have my "own agenda" when advising a Committee of the UK Parliament. That agenda was perceived to be the promotion of a new way to encourage dialogue and openness in politics. My appointment was not renewed. I accept the charge against me and the consequences that flow from it. However, I have lost a role where I could with more discretion perhaps have achieved more influence.

A question arose in our conference session which I had not fully considered before: does mediation sit within or outside "the system"? This may beg the question about what we mean by "the system". What if we mean the litigation system? Or the justice system? Or the western democratic system? At what point can we no longer answer the question with a yes or no? At what point is mediation inescapably part of the system?

Would those promoting an authoritarian, hierarchical, directive culture wish to engage in a process which tolerates, encourages, and even requires open-minded engagement and dialogue, with respect for all points of view? Should mediators engage with such authoritarian thinking at all? What if the very engagement might change people's approach? What if participation in mediation itself can never be "neutral" in its effects? What if mediation is, for some at least, destabilising? What if the authoritarians discover that mediation can be a Trojan horse for a liberal, consensual approach?

A final thought: Mediation itself may actually be an agent of change whether we like it or not and whether or not we hold ourselves out as merely impartial facilitators of a process. If that is so, should we make it compulsory?

Originally published in Kluwer Mediation Blog on 28 October 2018.

A Universal Declaration of Interdependence is Needed

Not long ago, I read a review of Yuval Noah Harari's new book, 21 Lessons for the 21st Century. The message contained in it was so stark that I found myself temporarily paralysed with fear about the future. I had a visceral sense of powerlessness against a coming tide of AI, automation, biotechnology, digital dictatorships, global warming and control by superior elites. No wonder we find ourselves distracted by relatively minor issues like Brexit and President Trump's behaviour. At least we can get our 20th century (or maybe just primitive?) minds around apparently everyday threats.

And then I read about The Perils of Perception by former Ipsos Mori managing director, Bobby Duffy. Duffy's thesis is that, statistically and empirically, things are much better than they have ever been. However, we humans suffer from serious delusion, are intuitively biased towards gloom, and hard-wired for pessimism as a defence mechanism dating back to the age when survival was largely about physical threats. But the resulting "miasma of misconception" seems almost as bad as Harari's predictions. The anonymity of the mob and populist fake news movements lead us into silos, echo chambers and other identity groups,

where we blame others for our "own and the world's misfortunes".

This feeling of hopelessness/helplessness led me to reflect on what we might do in our communities and countries to reassert our sense of identity as part of the whole – and how we might express our need for, and dependence on, each other, as an antidote to isolation and alienation.

Former UN Secretary General Kofi Annan, who died recently, placed considerable emphasis on the concept of global inter-dependence. This seems to resonate. So, I offer the idea of an Interdependence Day underscored by a Universal Declaration of Interdependence.

In the UK, for example, we might aim for an Interdependence Day in mid-March next year, just before we exit from the EU (if we do). This is not to assert that we should remain in the EU, whatever we may think individually, but to acknowledge that, in John Donne's words, "no man is an island". Indeed, we hear less frequently the fuller context: "No man is an island entire of itself; every man is a piece of the continent, a part of the main..."

Nor is this to say that we cannot be individuals and organise ourselves in ways which differentiate one from another. It's important to recognise diversity and difference – in aspirations, beliefs, purpose, values and our understanding of the way to live. Each of us is unique with our own special characteristics and traits, and we can never be one monolithic whole.

However, unless we are able to seal ourselves off hermetically from those we see as "others", we are not and cannot be truly independent of each other, whether as individuals or as groups. That conclusion has profound implications for policy, politics, and our individual and collective futures.

We really are interdependent. We need to work with each other, as individuals and peoples. Anything else is futile and self-defeating. Only by collaborating to improve our individual and collective lot will we manage to navigate through the stormy waters of this century.

Harvard Professor Martin Nowak writes in his book Super Cooperators that we need each other in order to succeed: "If we are to continue to thrive, we have but one option. ... We now have to refine and to extend our ability to cooperate. We must become familiar with the science of cooperation." Most effective mediators and negotiators know this well.

Nowak makes the point that, although we have much more in common than ever sets us apart, our species has tended to operate in tension, whether as individuals or as groups, with a selfish instinct leading to such global problems as climate change, environmental pollution, resource depletion, poverty, hunger and over-population. We can add those to Harari's list. And we must view all of this in the context of the danger of overstating, or misstating, the consequences.

The only way forward seems to be to articulate that which unites us, work together to overcome our differences and indeed make sacrifices for each other, in order to maximise our prospects of thriving – or even just surviving. So, maybe articulating the terms of a Universal Declaration of Interdependence is just what we need.

Originally published in The Scotsman on 29 October 2018.

The Certainties of the Past
Will No Longer Afford Security in the Future

"The only thing that will redeem mankind is cooperation" - Bertrand Russell

It is becoming more and more evident that a binary approach to important political questions is no longer fit for purpose. It is also fairly obvious that the certainties of the past will no longer afford security in the future. We live in an uncertain, ambiguous and somewhat paradoxical world.

And yet much of our contemporary political discussions are conducted as debates on the apparent assumption that there are right or wrong answers to complex problems and that, once certain decisions have been taken, no matter the basis for doing so, they cannot be reviewed in light of changed circumstances or new information.

This approach is deeply damaging, to our ability to cope with a complex world and to the reputation of those involved. In attempts to appear strong, those committed to dualist thinking undermine their position and lose ground. We need to find ways to enable our decision-making to be confidently nuanced, subject to change, provisional, open to multiple options, willing to adapt.

More than this, though, we need to come to terms with the notion that, just as no man is an island, no community, tribe, political party, nation or continent can exist without reference to others. Now, as perhaps never before, we are all inter-connected. The old boundaries, physical, political and psychological can no longer sustain separateness. Walls and borders cannot protect us in the way they might have done in the past.

This has profound implications for how we conduct political discussions and engage with others. To be "independent" in such a world probably makes no literal sense. To be in "union" with others in a diverse world where differences so clearly exist tends to create hierarchies and resentments, fear and anger, and may indeed perpetuate unhealthy dependence.

We need to transcend these strait-jackets which we impose linguistically and otherwise on our thinking and ability to act. The key may be to recognise our inevitable interdependence – our reliance on others alongside our own need to thrive.

In biology, mathematics and social science, we are being told that cooperation is the key to survival. Survival of the fittest in the sense of seeking to prevail over others by force (physical, psychological or political) is not, in the long run, a sustainable proposition. Ironically perhaps, if we skilfully help "the other", we will tend to help ourselves and optimise the outcomes for all. But this does need us to take a longer view rather than merely seeking relatively short-term notional victories which, if only in hindsight, will usually turn out to be pyrrhic or at best sub-optimal. In a zero-sum game, there are no real winners.

One of the problems in a binary world is that language is used which perpetuates and encourages polarity and antagonism. Argument becomes personal and offensive, creating its own downward spiral of abuse. Civility is the price paid with the concurrent loss of the ability to engage constructively in the public square.

Take two current examples of the impact of such positional politics:

(i) the effects of changes in the earth's climate will vary in different parts of the world. But overall, our species is threatened with significant and detrimental impacts which are likely to have implications globally for billions of people.

There is only one way to address this meaningfully and that is on a global scale and, yet, the interests of individual communities, nations or financial institutions are still dominant, creating division and increasing risk. Interdependence is the only platform for action which will be effective.

(ii) in the UK, there is a continuing controversy over the future of Scotland as a constituent part of the nation. The controversy is viewed as being "part of the union" or "independent" of it, with the referendum in 2014 cast in Yes/No terms. A similar approach underscored the debate over whether the UK should "remain" a part of the European Union or "leave". The difficulty in negotiating a satisfactory outcome after a "leave" vote illustrates well the superficiality of the question posed and the arguments offered.

"In" or "out", Scotland and the rest of the UK will remain closely intertwined, geographically, economically, culturally and linguistically. Our relationships will remain strong. While some links are less historically established, the same will be true generally with the rest of Europe, especially for young people. We are truly interdependent.

How can we work with these realities and build on them while acknowledging the growing need for multiple identities to be recognised?

How can we address modern separateness and difference while harnessing common interest and offering mutual support? How do we reduce our reliance on fear-based notions of "them" to provide our sense of security and identity, while enabling a view of "us" to be much more inclusive than we have hitherto tolerated? These questions can only be answered, it seems, by accepting that we must live interdependently. The pursuit of interdependence, as a stage in our collective development which takes us beyond dependence and independence, seems critical to our futures.

The time has surely come for an interdependence movement.

Originally published in The Scotsman on 14 June 2018.

Civility in Politics Should Not Be Too Much to Hope For

As many of us wrestle with the question of where to place our cross [in the General Election], perhaps we need to approach our choice differently.

Suppose we believe that the biggest concern is how we do politics, rather than any particular policy. Suppose we wish to see reform of public discourse and a return of civility. Suppose we see our politicians as bellwethers of how society discusses important matters. Suppose we think that civil discourse in parliament may be the essential precondition to a more mature consideration of what really matters, such as climate change, automation of jobs and mass migration, in addition to constitutional issues.

What sort of people do we wish to see and hear considering these and other difficult matters? How would we wish them to conduct themselves, and behave towards each other and others, including us, the electorate? We probably know the answers.

Might the answers give us relevant benchmarks for deciding how to vote? Suppose we vote for the candidates who show most respect towards people with different views. What

about those who go so far as to accept that nobody has a monopoly on the right way to do things?

What about the candidate who listens to other views and tries to answer questions directly and frankly? What about a candidate who exhibits humility and restraint? Would we give more credence to a candidate who avoids using inflammatory language and refuses to engage in personally derogatory remarks?

What about the candidate who behaves as we would expect other people in our workplace to behave towards us? Would we give weight to someone who looks to find common ground where possible on the really difficult issues, and who is transparent about why he or she differs on certain matters? Should we applaud a candidate who explains that binary choices don't reflect the complicated, volatile, ambiguous realities we face?

If thousands of us opted to use these criteria to decide our votes, might that affect the outcome? It's possible, especially if we declare our intentions. There are those who will say that this is naive. It's politics and the present state of things is just how we do it. I for one don't accept that.

There is precious little evidence to suggest that the present state of things is a credible way to continue. Indeed, it is hard to be confident about the future unless we embrace dignity and civility in political discourse in this country. It can hardly make things worse than they are. It might just make things better.

Originally published in The Times on 10 December 2019.

Post Election Reflections

The Scotsman newspaper asserted in its editorial on Saturday 14 December 2019 that "Humility, respect and compromise can be good politics". That is surely a welcome reflection on what now seems essential in our national life. Whatever our perspective, we must accept that, under the present system, there is an outcome to the general election process. We can acknowledge that, for many people, that outcome is not what they wished but it is nevertheless reality.

Those in positions of influence will be wise to recognise the impact of the result on people who hold diverse and deeply held points of view and to offer reassurance that they will seek positive ways forward. Paradoxically perhaps, finding as much common ground as possible in the interests of communities, businesses and individuals is a sure way to rebuild trust and confidence. After all, we need to live together.

All of this can be done without appearing to be weak on overall objectives and long-term goals. Ironically, perhaps, these may be more likely to succeed if short-term behaviour is as constructive as possible, while still being clear about what is important. Seductive though it may seem, things are rarely purely binary, black and white, right or wrong. A zero-sum game leaves no winners, only losers. We must override that.

Somehow, we have to expand the constitutional, social and economic pies in ways which are consistent with addressing the climate emergency. That will take imagination, empathy and wisdom. Great leaders have achieved great things in history by having the courage to shift from confrontation to cooperation. That is surely the challenge our leaders now face.

Originally published on Core's website on 18 December 2019.

Mediation in a Changing Climate? - From Consensus to Confrontation?

Opening Address given at the International Mediation Symposium of the Centre for International Legal Studies on 13 June 2019 at the Schloss Leopoldskron, Salzburg

It is a privilege to speak here in this wonderful place - what an appropriate setting when you read about the history and aspirations of the Salzburg Global Seminar - and to address you all in this opening session.

I'd like to start with some provocation. Imagine these alternatives to the usual headlines:

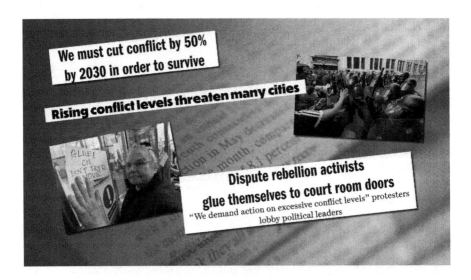

We must cut conflict by 50% by 2030 in order to survive

Rising conflict levels threaten many cities

Dispute rebellion activists glue themselves to court room doors

"We demand action on excessive conflict levels" protesters lobby political leaders

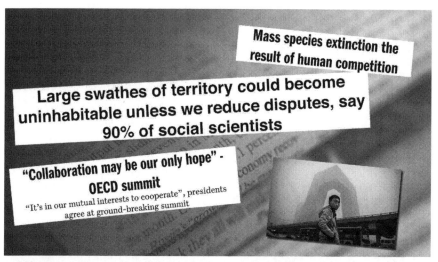

Mass species extinction the result of human competition

Large swathes of territory could become uninhabitable unless we reduce disputes, say 90% of social scientists

"Collaboration may be our only hope" - OECD summit
"It's in our mutual interests to cooperate", presidents agree at ground-breaking summit

Dispute avoidance economy creates thousands of jobs
Conflict management strategies contribute to 2% growth in economy

Mediation skills crucial to the future - UN report
Only mediators can save the world - experts say

Confirmation bias causes economic downturn
Recession attributable to fight or flight default setting, say neuroscientists
Wilful blindness costs economy millions, say finance ministers

Why not? Are these not just as valid as the usual headlines?

Three weeks ago, I was in Alaska with my wife, en route to a mediation conference in Banff, Alberta. We were on a cruise ship in Glacier Bay National Park surveying the staggering Margerie Glacier: our onboard nature guide told us that temperatures in Alaska had increased by 4 degrees in a generation, glaciers were receding and the permafrost was melting.

A few days later as we left Alberta, our view on take off was curtailed by thick smoke for hundreds of miles, caused by uncontrollable wild fires. These events are caused by climate change. The irony was not lost on us. We were of course contributing by being there. An uncomfortable cognitive dissonance.

All of this is yet further tangible evidence that we face a crisis.

That crisis represents an existential threat to our existence as a species.

It feels strange to say this so publicly. It has always seemed so distant, so unreal. I have been in partial denial I suppose and I still am. We probably all are.

But even in recent weeks, around the world, as the evidence mounts, and protests increase, many of us have come to accept that we face a climate emergency.

It is now something we have to face directly in our lives.

At the same time we are witnessing another degradation of our environment, this time of our political environment – throughout much at least of the western world.

I write this as Britain's planned exit from the European Union threatens to tear the country apart. Brexit has exposed the inability of the traditional process of parliamentary politics in the UK to address the increasingly complex issues of the 21st century, not least because my country, Scotland, presently an integral part of the UK, wishes to remain in the EU.

A process built on debate and division, on adversarial argument and binary voting on most issues, and founded on a party-political system which relies on positional and often parochial views, seems no longer suited to the complexities of the modern era.

Around the world, there is increasing populism and confrontation as many people seek to express their frustration and alienation. Traditional norms have been departed from and some very unpleasant polarisation is emerging.

Separateness and differentiation from others we don't like or feel uncomfortable with is becoming an increasingly acceptable trend, coupled with violence of language and apparent loss of decency and self-control.

This also all feels quite tangible. It's as if we've been collectively seized by Daniel Kahneman's System 1.

I am struck by these words of Tim Hicks, who I am delighted to be preceding here today, from his excellent book, Embodied Conflict, which could provide another of our alternative headlines:

"It's interesting to think about the violence we see in the world, whether at the level of interpersonal relationships, or at the societal and global levels, as a public health issue."

That further headline could read: "Relationship Violence is a Public Health Issue."

We seem to have gone from, or to be going from, consensus to confrontation. Who would have thought that, nearly 30 years after the Berlin Wall came down, the Soviet Union collapsed, Fukuyama wrote *The End of History* and *Getting to Yes* was published, we would be regressing as we seem to be. The climate is changing in more ways than one.

I picked up a book in the library here this morning: *World Without Borders* by Lester R Brown. Published in 1973, the author dedicates his book to *"a world order in which conflict and competition among nations will be replaced with cooperation and a sense of community."* The reviews featured on the back cover say that Brown *"persuasively argues...that the day of the militaristic-nation state is over, and that a unified global society is the only hope for survival."* and offers *"convincing evidence that the*

'One World' concept may be much closer to realisation than we are aware..". How far away that seems now.

If one adds rapid and widespread technological innovation, not least AI, eco-system and species breakdown, mass migration and other growing international tensions, making up what is known as the VUCA world (Volatile, Uncertain, Complex and Ambiguous), we have to ask if the conventional paradigm for political decision-making and policy-making is fit for purpose?

To that question we can add traditional ways of problem solving more generally, including of course our own world of dispute resolution.

Against that introductory background, I pose two related questions this morning:

Why is this relevant to us?

What should we do?

I would respond in this way:

I believe we mediators may hold, at least in part, a way to help to rebalance things, to move us back to the necessary state of collaboration without which our future as a species seems to be at great risk. There is no room for positional bargaining any more when it comes to the environmental risks. We're all in it together and an interest-based approach seems to be the only way to deal with it, not just a nice to have.

Martin Nowak, in his excellent book, *Super Cooperators*, reminds us that this fits with the prevailing evolutionary theme of cooperation. It's not about survival of the fittest, but the flourishing of the collaborative.

We know that adversarialism is costly. Whether in our justice systems, the way we handle disputes generally, national politics or international diplomacy, we must find ways to move away from binary, right/wrong, right/left, win/lose, in/out, yes/no decision making. Zero sum negotiation isn't fit for purpose.

We need a more enlightened, expansive, constructive, creative way to sort out our difficulties. This applies to prevention and reduction as well as to resolution

We need, in the jargon, to find durable, efficient, least damaging methods to reduce and resolve the effects of differences between people, groups and nations.

I might add, and I believe that it's not going too far to say this, that Tim Hicks' excellent analysis of neuro science describes what may be the missing piece in all of this, not least in helping us better to understand what happens to us and in our brains in situations of conflict - and what we might do about it.

I think it also provides us with clues as to why we may be reluctant to put ourselves forward, and why our attempts may be rebuffed. Risk aversion, inertia, fear of loss, resistance to change - all the familiar biases and blockers come into play.

However, I argue that our need to discover, or rediscover, consensual ways of handling difficult issues is, in this century, a matter of species survival. Unless we are able to really listen to each other, understand the deep underlying issues, explore the real needs and interests of people and of the planet, identify and develop creative options, use objective criteria to assess them, and help each other to make innovative decisions, our very futures are at risk.

What I have just described are of course classic attributes of effective mediation. As mediators, we have the knowledge and experience to offer a constructive way of doing things. We have a calling to help people to find resolution of the most intractable of disputes. We do it week in, week out.

My thesis is that this calling needs to be extended and offered at the highest levels now, in the biggest issues, in a really significant way.

Therefore we can and must use our skills, including our mediation skills and all we understand in that connection, to do what we can to help manage and resolve wider global issues, such as the impact of climate change and the polarisation of and within politics.

I pause to ask: what might this mean for you? Many of you are, I know, already engaged in policy and political work. How can that be extended? If you are not, what might you do?

And of course we must continue to refine what we already do to better help people to resolve their own local and individual disputes, in a sustainable and environmentally friendly way, in the broadest sense of that term.

Mediation offers just that, a sustainable and environmentally friendly way to deal with disagreement. That's why the topics of this conference are so important. We must do what we already do really well.

To refine this argument a little, one of the problems these days is that we seem to be outcome focused with insufficient attention to relationships and process. (I accept that this may be a western view, however, and that things may be different in other cultures.)

A wonderful writer in this field, known to many of you, Kenneth Cloke, emphasises in his latest book, Politics, Dialogue and the Evolution of Democracy, the criticality of these three components, which he describes as content, process and relationships. He bemoans the lack of attention to the latter two.

Cloke points out that nearly all of our focus in solving political problems is on content while comparatively little time is spent on process and relationships. As he points out, this may be fatal to solving seemingly intractable issues – like Brexit. As we know, working hard to build trust and goodwill, being careful with language and showing respect for contrary viewpoints, enhances rather than diminishes the prospects of success.

This is obvious perhaps. But, to an observer, this doesn't appear to be the experience in Brexit and in other major serious negotiations and we may all suffer the consequences. Perhaps there are exceptions in the work of leaders in our field like William Ury, for example in connection with the North Korean negotiations which averted, for a while at least, a potential major crisis.

In a similar vein to Cloke, in his book, *Negotiating the Impossible*, Deepak Malhotra describes three central components of effective negotiation in slightly different terms: framing, process and empathy. He says: *"In negotiations of all kinds, the greater your capacity for empathy – the more carefully you try to understand all of the other side's motivations, interests and constraints – the more options you tend to have for potentially resolving the dispute or deadlock."* These are wise words. He goes on to conclude that *"a lack of empathy usually guarantees failure."*

In mediation we have so much to offer, in helping protagonists to consider not just the content and the substantive issues but also the framework or process for negotiations, together with the necessary glue to make it all work – effective working relationships. That's our job. Politicians and policy makers need this very much. They need impartial, skilled, wise, thoughtful third siders to support them to create effective processes and to build rapport and empathy.

In conclusion, I accept that all this may seem rather naive and might not be enough in all cases.

Tim Hicks would tell us that we might need to use rights and power also. In the case of climate change, he says, the urgency of our situation calls for every effort at every level. If we can find opportunities for dialogue and consensus-building, we should pursue those. But progress via that avenue on its own will likely be too slow. Work in the courts and on the streets also seems necessary he argues.

So be it. The crisis is urgent and extremely serious. But that does mean that we must work hard on, as Tim describes it, dialogue and consensus-building. On what we do as mediators. It's what we have to offer. It's our contribution.

We must ensure that we play our part in addressing, and bring our skills to trying to solve, the most intractable problems.

That is surely our calling.

A Changing World

"The only thing that will redeem mankind is cooperation"

Since compiling this book, we have begun to experience the unprecedented coronavirus pandemic. The following pieces, each building on the quotation above, reflect on its impact.

Love Over Fear – and Holding on to Hope

"The only thing which will redeem mankind is cooperation" said the philosopher Bertrand Russell. Perhaps only a real crisis will enable us truly to appreciate what this means and what it takes.

The impact of the COVID-19 virus is seen by some to be akin to being in a world war though, as others have observed, military metaphors seem unhelpful. The extent of disruption may in fact be more extensive for many people. On this occasion, however, we are all in it together. There is a common threat. We cannot overwhelm it by force. We do need to help each other, to find a vaccine, to reduce the risk of infection, to provide support to those afflicted and so on.

Unless we choose to look for scapegoats, there is no us and them. This time, with a very few exceptions, no man or woman is an island. While we must do what we can to reduce transmission, physical borders and walls are a partial protection only to keep out that which threatens us.

Maybe, just maybe, this provides us with the very opportunity we need. Hubris and manipulation will have limited traction. Humility and honesty are the only currency. Leaders are emerging who manifest these

qualities. The rest of us have choices. When we are fearful, the natural reaction may be to retreat into self-protection. Fight, flight or freeze. But we'll need to try and override that understandable impulse.

Thinking about the needs of others as well as ourselves will take conscious thought, compassion and kindness. That is what we need to do to survive, to get through this. What is in your interests is also likely to be in mine. What might that mean in families, in communities and in our nations? How does that fit with staying at home? It is in our mutual interests to reduce contact as much as possible. Can we find ways where minimal contact can be balanced with being, somehow, available to others, while still adhering to official instructions?

How we resolve such apparent dilemmas may be some of the biggest challenges in this whole experience. Let's keep asking questions and listening to others to ascertain their needs, hopes and fears. Let's acknowledge these and try to offer appropriate reassurance and help. Let's explore what we can realistically do for each other. Let's ensure that love prevails over fear.

Above all, let's hold on to hope. The hope of a future where we recognise that we – and the planet which sustains us – are interdependent, vulnerable and much in need of cooperation in order to survive.

Originally published in Kluwer Mediation Blog on 28 March 2020.

World Leaders Must Set Aside Rivalry to Fight This Scourge

"The only thing which will redeem mankind is co-operation," observed the philosopher Bertrand Russell. Perhaps only a real crisis is enabling us truly to appreciate what this means and what it might take.

What if one of our world leaders wrote to their counterparts in the following terms: "We face unprecedented times. None of us could have imagined these events a few months ago. I write to you with a plea for global co-operation. I acknowledge that we have real differences among us which makes even considering co-operation very difficult."

"I accept that the reality of the world we have all lived in means it is hard to imagine how we could work together. We have often behaved in a competitive way and said or done things which provoke each other. We have each tended to place our own nations' interests before wider needs."

"However, we have never before been so globally connected, nor have we faced a collective crisis like this where disease has spread so rapidly across the planet. This calls for an exceptional response, a response of a different order from anything we have contemplated before."

"We are all in this together. There is a common threat. We cannot overwhelm it by force. The only way both to overcome this threat to our common humanity and to rebuild our economies is to work together. The only way to get back on our feet quickly is to help each other. That means sharing information about this disease, trying to find a vaccine together, and pooling our technical knowledge about how to prevent it, minimise it and protect ourselves."

"We must not take advantage of this only to serve our own interests. We will all gain if we combine. If we don't, we will at best have a sub-optimal outcome and, at worst, end up in what the economists call a zero-sum game. I fear we would all be losers. Our people deserve better than that."

"How can we deal with this on a global basis? I am sure there are a number of options. We must identify these and find the best way forward, calling on the expertise available to us all. May I suggest that we schedule an online meeting as soon as possible to begin?"

"We are expected to be leaders. In the interests of our common humanity, let us exercise that leadership in a new and constructive way."

"Above all, let us hold on to hope. The hope of a future where we recognise that we, and the planet which sustains us, are interdependent, vulnerable and much in need of co-operation in order to survive."

A pipe dream? Or humankind's only redemption?

Originally published in The Times on Tuesday 21 April 2020.

(Note: I am aware that the use of the word "mankind" is perceived by many as inappropriate. I acknowledge that concern. I felt it inappropriate to change the actual quotation from Russell. However, in using "humankind" in the last sentence above, I hope at least to have recognised how significant the use of language can be.)

Communication More Important Than Ever

I have been writing articles for the Scotsman law pages for many years. Occasionally it has been difficult to find a topic or a theme. But this must be the most difficult of all. What does one say which has any meaning at a time like this?

I've been wrestling with what mediators can offer in the current uncertainty. I have devoted myself to the mediation cause for nearly twenty years because I believe in it. I believe in it because it nearly always brings out the best in people and helps them to move on to a different stage in their lives whatever may have been troubling them. It offers a buffer to absorb negative emotions and a bridge to a more constructive future. Done well, it helps people to acknowledge what has gone wrong, to accept the reality that things are not always as we wish them to be and that others may see things differently.

Mediation recognises the impact of adverse events and tries to find a way for people to offer reassurance wherever possible that there is a way ahead. It encourages people to explore what is really worrying them, to identify their underlying concerns and needs and to identify and assess the realistic options which are available. From that very often emerges a way forward with which people can live, not perfect but manageable and durable.

Mediation works of course on the principle that we gain more if we help each other. Paradoxically perhaps, if I try to meet your needs, it is likely that, over the long term, I shall gain also. Never has that been more true than now. We are truly interdependent. We need each other more than ever, even while we are socially distant. The zero-sum game of winning and losing is an easy fallback in times of stress but ultimately it usually leads to losses for all.

What can we do? We know that the current situation will produce disputes and conflicts of all sorts. We know that there will be many unresolved issues which have preceded this time of sudden change. All of us associated with the legal profession can look out for opportunities to help others who have hit a difficulty. Not just in the conventional way which has been part of our business model but in new and creative ways. What front line could we be on?

How about contacting all clients and offering a listening ear on the phone? Many will be doing just that already. What sort of toolkit might be useful?

Are there essential skills for handling difficult conversations for example? Of course there are.

I offer here are a few tips to use and to pass on. They just might make a difference at the margins. Every little counts, especially when the enormity of the big picture is so hard to contemplate.

Ask questions that get under the surface: How are you? What is worrying you most? How can I help? What realistically can you do? Listen really well: when under pressure we can so easily jump in and express our own thoughts. People may just need our silence and full attention. Then we can acknowledge and accept what we hear and recognise another person's experience for what it is.

Be careful with language: under pressure, we may rush to say things which we don't really mean or which come across as unhelpful. Pause for a second or two and let the conscious mind formulate the words with as much compassion as we can muster. Remember that, even in this crisis, we may see things differently from others - not because we are good or bad, right or wrong, but because we are human, with all the vulnerabilities, assumptions and even prejudices that make us who we are.

And very pragmatically, make use of the online technology which opens up new avenues for communication for mediators and advisers alike. We are finding that a silver lining is the ability to continue to offer to help our clients by using the online platform Zoom, for example, relatively easily and in many ways ideal for this quite remarkable time.

We need to continue to find ways to offer hope and help. To do that, we must continue to communicate. And if we are not sure what to say, let's just say the kindest thing.

Originally published in The Scotsman on Monday 30 March 2020.

Printed in Great Britain
by Amazon

21244871R00052

Mediation / Conflict Resolution

A Mediator's Musings

on Mediation, Negotiation, Politics and a Changing World

As the founder and senior mediator of Core and a door tenant with Brick Court Chambers in London, John Sturrock QC has pioneered mediation and high quality negotiation and conflict management training and coaching in business, the professions, politics and sport.

He has been involved in hundreds of mediations covering a broad range of disputes in the public, private, policy and not for profit sectors in the UK, mainland Europe, Middle East and Africa. Who's Who Legal has listed John as a Global Elite Thought Leader and he is a Distinguished Fellow of the international Academy of Mediators.

For many years, he has worked with various parliamentary bodies throughout the UK on effective scrutiny of policy. He is also founder of Collaborative Scotland (www.collaborativescotland.org), which promotes non-partisan respectful dialogue about difficult issues. He writes regular blog posts and newspaper articles.

"John Sturrock's outstanding new book, 'A Mediator's Musings,' is much more powerful than its' humble title suggests. It is by turns profound and poignant, insightful and useful, current and lasting."

Kenneth Cloke, author of The Dance of Opposites: Explorations in Mediation, Dialogue and Conflict Resolution Systems Design

ISBN 9798640163988

9 798640 163988

9 0 0

Everybody Sharts

Written and Illustrated by John G.